The Business Value Web

Resourcing

DATE DUE

Business Processes

and Solutions in

Higher Education

Donald M. Norris & Mark A. Olson

NACUBO

National Association of College and
University Business Officers
Washington, DC
www.nacubo.org

ISBN 1-56972-026-6

Foreword by Peter C. McKenzie

On campuses across the country, the meeting of the governing board finance committee plays out in similar fashion: We sit around a large conference table with a dedicated group of alumni of our institutions who are frequently CEOs of major corporations. Inevitably the conversation turns to process improvement, cost reductions, or change management. The chief financial officer spends a good portion of the meeting gamely trying to explain that accomplishing these tasks is very challenging in a higher education environment where collegiality and consensus management reign. I've often used the analogy of a large ship in describing campus change: We can't turn on a dime and often we need the strong push of the tugboat to get us moving. Coming from "Corporate America" where rapid change, continuous improvement, and performance measurement are expected, our trustees don't doubt our sincerity to move the boat forward. But they do question whether we have the right tools and management structures in place to meet these challenges.

In the mid 1990s, 11 CFOs in the greater Boston area formed The Boston Consortium for Higher Education to look more directly at the management tools and practices that our institutions employed. We believed, like our governing board members, that we could better manage our institutions and enhance quality. While our trustees were certainly pushing the boat, other factors provided propulsion: declining enrollments, reduced federal funding, and escalating costs. Our belief in better management through leveraging our joint procurement capabilities, the collective talent of our staffs, and training and learning opportunities needed to be tested. As you will see in the following pages, the early test results are very positive.

NACUBO has also been a major catalyst for learning and development of higher education business practices. Training sessions offered to business officers have frequently taken new management practices developed for the corporate sector and tailored them to the specific needs of the higher education audience. NACUBO, in collaboration with Don Norris and Mark Olson, has produced another fine management text – *The Business Value Web*.

In the following pages, the business officer will explore with the authors how we can systematically look at our business processes, find new solutions for improving our business practices, and in that process create real value from our investment. The format of methodology background, case study, and practical next steps makes for a straightforward read. The case studies in particular point the business officer to examples of solutions that have achieved a valuable return on investment for our colleagues, today. The perspective on future developments focuses on new approaches to resourcing that will be possible over the next five years or sooner.

For those of us who need that little push every so often, Don Norris and Mark Olson propel us forward in *The Business Value Web*. We are in a period of great change. Therefore, experimentation, or an expeditionary approach as our authors describe it, is essential to our success in managing in these complex times.

Peter C. McKenzie is financial vice president and treasurer at Boston College. He currently serves as chairman of The Boston Consortium for Higher Education.

Table of Contents

INTRODUCTION

Resourcing Business Processes and Solutions in Higher Education

- *What is Value and Where Does it Reside?*
- *The Business Value Web*
- *New Opportunities for Resourcing*
- *Who Should Read This Book?*

Today's higher education business, auxiliary, and administrative services officers are on the front lines of enhancing the quality and controlling the costs of their institution's business processes. In particular, the chief business officer has an informed, institution-wide perspective of the interplay of institutional processes and finances. This is a unique vantage point from which to assess the performance of the institution's portfolio of business processes, services, and solutions and to suggest new approaches to their resourcing. The chief business officer must understand where value resides and how to enhance it.

This topic could not be more timely. Higher education is experiencing what's been described as "the perfect economic storm" caused by the unfortunate confluence of falling endowment returns; decreases in state funding; increasing costs for financial aid, health premiums, and energy; and a number of other forces. At the same time, advances in business process outsourcing, shared services, and the technologies for deconstructing and stitching together business processes enable fresh approaches to resourcing. Institutions face significant opportunities to change the way they do business.

To help understand where value resides and how to enhance it, we have created the framework of the business value web. Using fresh approaches to resourcing and organizational development, business officers will increasingly be called upon to participate in deconstructing and reinventing the business value web at their institutions.

What Is Value and Where Does It Reside?

Shrewd leadership is needed to leverage the elements of value found in colleges and universities.

Value is the benefit derived from an enterprise's assets by its stakeholders. For colleges and universities, value is derived by students, faculty, staff, other knowledge seekers, alumni, donors, suppliers, and stakeholders. They derive value through experiencing the institution's programs, services, knowledge assets, and other resources. The gateways for experiencing these assets and deriving value are the multitude of academic and administrative processes through which the institution engages its stakeholders. Institutions that achieve a superior value proposition can experience a competitive advantage over others.

Value is a combination of quality and price; it involves both outcomes and the nature of experience through which products, services, and assets are engaged. Even though we have ways of measuring quality or reputation and cost/price, value is relative rather than absolute. Value has limitless potential: productivity enhancement, innovation, reinvention, and creative combination can always be used to further

enhance the value proposition for colleges and universities.

Enterprises enhance the value experienced by stakeholders in a mixture of ways and at a variety of levels. They build the fundamental quality of their programs and services. They use leadership and strategies to enhance and leverage resources and to develop infrastructures and the capacities of individual faculty and staff. Finally, academic and administrative processes are improved and streamlined to support the programs, services, and other resources.

For years, savvy business officers have been helping their institutions to enhance their value proposition by investing shrewdly in programs, people, infrastructures, leadership, strategies, and processes. They have come to understand the value of synergy between the different contributors. Able leadership has enabled institutions to establish competitive advantage not just by spending more than other institutions but also by leveraging the different elements of value.

Elements of Value

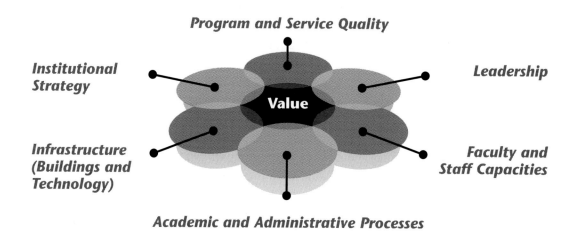

Program and Service Quality

Institutional Strategy

Leadership

Value

Infrastructure (Buildings and Technology)

Faculty and Staff Capacities

Academic and Administrative Processes

The Business Value Web

Value

Value resides in the interstices between knowledge, learning, research, service, and the collaborative endeavors of university communities. Like energy, value is both potential and kinetic. It exists in many states and places in a sort of "value web." Like the tension in a spring, value is elastic and propels the growth of knowledge and learning exchange.

Enterprises of all kinds have found that the Knowledge Economy changes their value proposition in fundamental ways. Many vectors of value are based on communication, interactivity, and the sharing/experiencing of knowledge. Information and communications technology (ICT) is the enabler, facilitator, and accelerator of many existing products, services, processes, and experiences. New sources of value are emerging from what was once considered the "soft" side of business - collaboration, innovation, knowledge management, business process reinvention, communities of practice, and productivity enhancement.

As these developments continue, the traditional concept of a "value chain" is being replaced by the notion of a "value web." Value is not built by linear progression along tightly coupled process paths, but by drawing from resources and assets loosely connected through flexible relationships and interfaces.

Over time, business officers will understand and utilize this "business value web" as they work to optimize and leverage the value proposition provided by their institutions. They will use both "return on investment" (ROI) and "value on investment" (VOI) to guide their efforts.

New Opportunities for Resourcing

Resourcing provides new opportunities to connect and leverage people, processes, and systems from a variety of internal and external sources. This can maximize value while minimizing investment of scarce resources.

Just as the tools of the Knowledge Economy are opening new vectors of value for business officers to consider, they are revolutionizing the range of business process solutions that are available. A complex array of options has come to market including privatization of auxiliary services, IT outsourcing, business process outsourcing, application service providers, expert services, shared services, and process reinvention. Leading technology companies have elevated their status from "vendor" to "solution provider." Web services are enabling the seamless integration of loosely coupled services for parts of business processes. These changes require that the business officer be more vigilant than ever in separating hype from reality.

The business officer is now engaged in "resourcing" business processes and solutions in a manner that blends elements of value from a variety of sources. It's no longer a simple matter of "insourcing" or "outsourcing" but determining the blended, reinvented solution that will optimize and leverage every business process, alone and in combination with others. Traditional business analysis will increasingly demand a new approach, characterized by the "deconstruction" of business processes and the realignment of functional inputs and outputs, in innovative and inventive new configurations.

The current state of financial exigency confronting higher education promises to make resourcing decisions ever more complex and important. Institutions are aggressively seeking cost savings, productivity enhancements, and ways of creating genuine synergies that add value and distinctiveness. Chief business officers and administrative officers are stewards of institutional portfolios of business processes, which present significant opportunities for enhancement through clever resourcing decisions. The chief business officer is poised to become the most effective spokesperson for the cross-disciplinary teams that will craft strategies for optimizing value from institutional resources and reinventing processes.

Who Should Read This Book?

This book is essential reading for chief business officers and auxiliary services officers who are stewards of key business processes. Trustees, presidents, provosts, and other campus executives and managers, however, also need to understand:

- The strategic imperative of maximizing and leveraging value to establish competitive advantage

- The new sources of value and the emergence of the business value web

- Resourcing business processes and solutions to achieve process reinvention and services enhancement using a range of tools and approaches

- Determining who should participate in managing the campus solutions portfolio, and how this should be accomplished

- How to raise campus IQ about potential ROI and VOI from resourcing and reinvention of options and decisions

The current state of financial hardship in higher education will make this book required reading in colleges and universities.

The Evolution of Outsourcing, Shared Services, and Process Reinvention

CHAPTER 1

- *Privatization and Outsourcing*
- *Shared Services*
- *Process Reinvention*
- *Enter Resourcing*

Over the past 40 years, colleges and universities have developed extensive experience with outsourcing and privatizing auxiliary services, information technology, and entire business processes. As experience and sophistication have grown, the scope, length, and complexity of privatization arrangements have expanded as well. New providers have emerged and the nature of the relationships between institutions and outsourcing partners has evolved. Business process outsourcing has increased, delegating the management of a wide range of business processes, both administrative and academic, to third-party providers. Web services enable processes to be deconstructed, resourced, and seamlessly reintegrated. Today's difficult financial climate has elevated the importance of these issues.

Shared services and process reinvention have been critical ingredients in the value proposition offered by outsourcing providers. In addition, many institutions have used these tools to improve the efficiency and quality of processes and services that they have continued to provide in-house.

All of these practices fall under the rubric of resourcing, which describes the practice of developing multi-faceted solutions for the institution's business processes. These blended solutions add and release value to the institution. They aim to reduce costs and enhance the quality of products, services, and experiences. All of the institution's processes are candidates for changes in their resourcing mix and innovation, to create new kinds of value. Business, auxiliary, and administrative services officers are emerging as leaders in determining where value resides and leveraging that value to establish competitive advantage. They are key players in the cross-functional teams that are evaluating the institution's portfolio of processes for continuous improvement and value enhancement.

Terms and Concepts

Business Processes: Encompasses everything from academic affairs and auxiliary operations to zoological collections. Back-office, front-office, teaching, research, and public services are all involved.

Business Process Outsourcing (BPO): The delegation of one or more resource-intensive business process to an external provider, who controls and manages the selected processes based on measurable performance metrics.

Business Process Reengineering (BPR): The use of knowledge management tools to streamline processes, reducing costs and enhancing productivity. BPR is not a term with which higher education is comfortable.

Collaboration: Formal and informal working together and sharing of ideas and insights. True collaboration is a key competency for today's successful solution seeker.

Competencies and Culture for Collaborative Solutions: A multiple-partner solution environment requires new competencies and changes in the organizational culture.

Deconstruction and Reinvention of Business Processes: Technology enables institutions to deconstruct their current approaches to business processes and reinvent them. The results are productivity enhancement, process efficiency, and improved service and customer satisfaction.

Expert Services: Technical, process, and practice expertise provided by consultants, technology providers, and solution providers. These expert services include insights continuously drawn from other clients and shared.

Fusion of Academic and Administrative Processes: The distinctions between academic and administrative processes are history. In today's environments, the two are **fused**, not just integrated.

Information Technology Outsourcing (ITO): Focuses on outsourcing various aspects of information and communications technology infrastructures and services.

Privatization and Outsourcing: Using external providers to furnish particular services and/or processes. Higher education has extensive experience with outsourcing and privatization of a variety of campus services – bookstores, food services, residence halls, buildings and grounds, IT facilities management, and other auxiliary services.

Resourcing: The blend of shared, expert, on-campus and off-campus services necessary to create business processes and solutions for higher education institutions.

Service Level Agreement: Agreed upon service levels for business process outsourcing.

Shared Services: Those services and/or solutions that are shared by multiple units within a single enterprise, or across multiple enterprises. Shared services are provided through institutional consortia, an application service provider (ASP) relationship with a solution provider, or a BPO relationship.

Solutions: In the new Web environment, institutions are paying more for services than software. Moreover, they are ultimately seeking solutions, not just technology. Outsourcing partners are seen as solution providers, not vendors.

Privatization and Outsourcing

Higher education institutions have extensive experience contracting with private companies to provide a variety of services. This practice, called privatization or outsourcing, enables institutions to focus attention on core activities, save money on the provision of non-core services, and/or improve the quality of a campus service that had diminished due to lack of leadership or ineffective management. Over time, three distinct aspects of outsourcing have emerged: privatization of auxiliary and other revenue-generating services, IT outsourcing, and business process outsourcing (BPO).

Privatization of Auxiliary and Other Revenue Generating Services

The National Association of College Auxiliary Services (NACAS) supported a number of surveys in the late 1990s, conducted by Richard Wertz, that captured the state-of-the-art of outsourcing, primarily of auxiliary services. The following table illustrates the palette of auxiliary and ancillary services that traditionally have been outsourced by colleges and universities.

Privatization Profile of Services

Services Typically Privatized
Campus travel agencies; Asbestos removal projects; Drink and snack food machines; Refuse and waste management; Hazardous waste removal; Video game machines; Banking services; Food service; Construction projects; Student laundry machines; Research waste removal; Textbook publishing; Architectural and engineering services

Services Privatized by 20 to 60 Percent of Those Surveyed
Beauty salon/operations; Student loan collections; Retail store/shopping areas; Worker's compensation programs; Retirement programs; Bookstore; Auditing and accounting; Employee assistance programs; Tuition plans; Unemployment compensation; Copier machines; Printing and publications; Trademarks and licensing; Games/amusement center; Golf courses; Athletic concessions; Physical plant financing; Housing facility building; Day care centers; Campus future planning; Housekeeping; Energy conservation; Recycling programs; Real estate development/operations

Services Rarely Privatized or Privatized by Less than 20 Percent of Those Surveyed
Payroll services; Law enforcement and safety; Security; Employee training programs; Student health centers; Faculty clubs; Press; Grounds; Health and safety services; Parking garage; Benefits administration/operations; Maintenance; Parking administration/enforcement; Classification/compensation; Campus mail service; Student counseling centers; Motor pool operations; Conference center management; Recreational areas/camps; Coliseum/arena management; Conference centers; Cinemas/theaters; Computer operations; Housing operations; Identification card production; Institutional research; Student union operations; Student housing staff/programs; Career counseling center operations; Placement center operations; Student financial aid services; Fund raising and development; Admissions; Student activities

Source: Richard Wertz, 1997.

Richard Wertz is a recognized authority on outsourcing, having written the definitive books on the subject for the National Association of College Auxiliary Services. He has 20 years' experience as vice president and director of business affairs at the University of South Carolina.

The Wertz Survey also captured the key reasons for outsourcing and the concerns about privatizing/outsourcing services on campus, from a group of 932 institutions. Cost savings and improving quality of services were far and away the primary reasons for considering outsourcing, each being cited by over half the respondents. On the other hand, nearly four out of 10 respondents expressed concern over loss of control and inability to manage the contractor, followed closely by "service quality/inconsistency in customer satisfaction" (31%) and "employee displacement or morale (24%)."

The drivers of outsourcing are primarily related to ROI, whereas the concerns about outsourcing tend to focus on the value dimension. The business value web model provides the means for reconciling drivers and concerns. In particular, alleviating concerns about loss of control come through enhancing trust.

These analyses painted a picture of the pros and cons of outsourcing of services by the late 1990s. But changes in internal and external drivers in recent years have led to significant growth in the scope of outsourcing in higher education.

Reasons for/Concerns about Outsourcing of Services

Primary Reasons for Considering Outsourcing			Concerns About Outsourcing		
Reason	#	%	Concern	#	%
1. Cost savings and budget constraints	739	79	1. Loss of control, ability to manage contractor	382	41
2. Improve quality of services, staffing, products	479	51	2. Service quality, customer satisfaction inconsistency	285	31
3. Contractor expertise, professional management, or better technology	137	15	3. Employee displacement or morale	220	24
4. Lack capability/skilled workers to provide services or rural locations	76	8	4. Impersonal nature, loss of identity, community, culture, collegiality	109	12
5. Safety concerns or liability of service	76	8	5. Union demands, existing labor contracts, state regulations	94	10
6. Staffing difficulties, problems in eliminating employees	35	4	6. Mission of institution, loss of loyalty, no longer term commitment	72	8
7. Improved focus on core programs or relocate resources	29	3	7. Fear of contractor not being able to respond to campus change	46	5
8. Market competition or capital investment	20	2	8. Fear of lack of knowledgeable administrators and management skills by contractor	28	3
9. Reduce personnel benefits, avoid discriminatory practices	19	2	9. Contractor financial strength	19	2
			10. Renewal costs, re-start-up costs if contractor does not work out	19	2
Source: Richard Wertz, 1997			11. Profits lost to outsiders	8	1

Wertz (2003) recently identified the issues in outsourcing and privatization that are facing higher education:

- *Dealing with and/or preventing bankruptcy issues with vendors.* Protecting colleges and universities from companies at risk of default and bankruptcy has become a real concern given the demise of application service providers (ASPs), e-learning companies, and other dot.com outsourcing partners. Many business officers have been forced to deal with such issues, before, during, and after bankruptcy.

- *Added importance of the request for proposal (RFP) and contract process.* Building appropriate RFPs, contracts, and measurement criteria/performance indicators has become an important success factor for outsourcing relationships. The client and outsourcing partner need to jointly develop a *service level agreement* that enables successful operations, performance measurement, joint oversight, and continuous improvement. Institutions need to develop far better levels of comprehension of the service levels and cost dimensions of their processes and services.

- *Growth in multi-campus contracts.* Recent outsourcing arrangements have expanded to include multi-campus systems. For example, Penn State University outsourced its bookstores for its 24 campuses statewide. Multi-unit contracts are likely to grow in the future.

- *Length of contract.* Many outsourcing partners are seeking extended contracts, 5-7 years or more, and up to 10-15 years if renovation funds are involved.

- *Outsourcing companies are investing in higher education.* Many outsourcing firms are making serious financial commitments to support outsourcing opportunities.

For example, Barnes & Noble built a free-standing facility at the University of Pennsylvania in Philadelphia.

- *Dangers of becoming "corporate-sponsored academia."* The sorts of lucrative, exclusive arrangements being sought by companies such as Coca Cola and Pepsi are raising values issues in the context of the structure of corporate sponsorship.

- *Responding to financial exigency.* State financial deficits have led to budget cuts, layoffs, and desperate searches for new ways to save money at public institutions. As a result, interest in outsourcing is growing, and partnering is critical because the states and institutions have no front-end money to invest in developing outsourcing arrangements or infrastructures. Private institutions have also responded to losses in endowment income and the increasing price sensitivity of parents.

- *Rising student expectations.* Students expect better service and amenities – this is becoming a key factor for many selective institutions, both public and private.

- *Diversity of outsourcing providers.* Colleges and universities are dealing with a broad range of outsourcing providers for auxiliary services and processes. They range from large firms offering auxiliary services outsourcing (Barnes & Noble, Sodhexo, Aramark), to franchise operations (Burger King, Chick Fil-A, Little Dinos) to local markets and merchants (flower shops, boutiques, other specialty providers).

Where will higher education privatization be in five years? Wertz expects resourcing arrangements to grow in complexity and scope and to spread throughout auxiliary service functions and many academic and administrative support functions, as well.

"The future of resourcing is that it will grow immensely. Without being a proponent as such, the fact remains that we must figure out how to provide services at high quality and low cost, and where should we look for opportunities. Nobody is going to be isolated. One must always be looking for different instruments, such as resourcing and partnering."

Richard Wertz

He foresees that public and private institutions alike will aggressively seek greater quality and reduced costs through resourcing activities (Wertz, 2003).

The EDUCAUSE Center for Applied Research (ECAR) studies leading edge issues relating to the deployment of information and communications technology in higher education.

Information Technology Outsourcing

In the 1960s and 1970s, IT outsourcing was called "facilities management," and by the 1980s and 1990s it had been labeled "systems operations." Moreover, "time sharing" and "contracting for services" have been familiar concepts in higher education for years. In 2002, the EDUCAUSE Center for Applied Research (ECAR) conducted a survey on the state-of-the-art of IT outsourcing. This study found that the level of IT outsourcing in higher education lagged behind that of other sectors. Nevertheless, the study found that:

- Forty two percent of colleges and universities engaged in ASP and/or IT outsourcing.

- Real or perceived lack of in-house skills was the overwhelming key driver of the IT outsourcing decision.

- IT outsourcing is distributed among segments such as IT infrastructure, application management, and application services.

- While 46 percent of public institutions report that e-learning and distance learning activities are suitable candidates for outsourcing, only 31 percent of private institutions share this perspective.

- About one-third of all survey respondents are considering insourcing (bringing back in-house) functions currently outsourced. (Both public and private institutions held similar perspectives.)

The ECAR Survey examined the following IT-supported/related functions that are outsourced: e-learning/distance education, processing services, network services, distributed systems, application services, application management, IT infrastructure, process services, and business process outsourcing. ECAR estimates the IT outsourcing market in higher education at $505 million in 2001 and forecasts it as growing at a compounded annual growth rate (CAGR) of 19 percent to $1.3 billion between 2001 and 2006.

This IT outsourcing forecast is based on a set of assumptions about the drivers and inhibitors shaping the deployment of IT outsourcing in higher education. The table on page 7 summarizes the survey's profile of these drivers and inhibitors.

IT outsourcing in higher education is projected to grow to $1.3 billion by 2006.

U.S. Higher Educational Operational Services Market By Segment, 2001-2006

Operational Services Segment	2001 (millions)	2006 (millions)	CAGR 2001-2006 percentage
IT Outsourcing			
IT Infrastructure Services	58	333	36%
Application Management	90	163	10%
Application Services	115	207	11%
Distributed Services	80	150	12%
Network Services	101	209	14%
E-Learning	61	256	29%
Total IT Outsourcing	**505**	**1,318**	**19%**
Business Process Outsourcing	158	336	14%
Process Services	119	276	16%
Total Operational Services	**782**	**1,930**	**17%**

Source: ECAR Survey, 2002, p. 76.

IT Outsourcing in Higher Education

Drivers	Inhibitors
• Pressure on budgets for both capital and operating costs	• Reluctance to incur risk, especially relating to dependence on vendors in a volatile industry
• Shift to Web-based technologies	• Risk of expensive litigation in case an outsourcing relationship sours
• Integration of IT technologies into operations functions, rather than in a supporting role	• Insufficient internal leadership to overcome inevitable internal resistance
• Scarce IT architectural and engineering staff resources	• Inability to undertake large, multiyear outsourcing commitments because of fiscal uncertainties or restrictions
• Various competitive pressures expressed through administrative, academic, education, and research demands	• Immature IT outsourcing solutions from vendors without sufficient higher education experience
	• Fewer role models than exist in the commercial or government sectors
	• Resistance to outsourcing by organized labor

Source: ECAR Survey, 2002, pp. 73-75.

The ECAR Study takes an evenhanded approach in assessing the pluses and minuses of IT outsourcing in higher education and the prospects for future growth. Despite the inhibitors, institutions have no choice but to include outsourcing of selected IT functions and services as one of the key elements of their resourcing options.

"The choice for institutions wishing to remain competitive through IT innovation will likely be between focused or widespread IT outsourcing, rather than between IT outsourcing or not. Clearly, even our most prestigious research universities are outsourcing, albeit at the margins of innovations. In a very sound strategy to rapidly acquire technology skills and to then assimilate those skills organizationally, research universities appear to outsource as an IT skill augmentation strategy."

Richard Katz, ECAR Research Report, Volume I 2002, p. 6-7.

The process of evaluating processes and functions for different approaches to resourcing and value enhancement is a valuable act in itself. It enables institutional leadership to assess where the true business value resides and how to improve performance. As technology is fused into processes, it also enables leadership to deconstruct and reinvent processes, forging new relationships with other institutions and resourcing partners.

"Ultimately, the promise and risk of outsourcing will impel higher education to rethink many of its organizational assumptions and practices. Why? Because outsourcing serves to disaggregate functions that were previously held tightly and forces managers to adopt ever more creative partnering relationships."

Ellen Hassett, Peter Cunningham, Emillia Kancheva, Matt Newsome, Sara Wells, ECAR Research Report, Volume I 2002, p.21.

Business process outsourcing will increase in higher education as loosely coupled systems and processes make it easier to deconstruct and resource particular parts of processes.

The Growth of Business Process Outsourcing

Among the greatest opportunities for growth in outsourcing lies in the use of information and communications technology (ICT) to change the dynamics and performance of organizational processes. This is called business process outsourcing (BPO).

"BPO is, very simply, the outsourcing of mission-critical, non-core business processes. These processes are prerequisites to achieving excellence in core operations, but are not competitive differentiators to an organization. Some companies and agencies get so bogged down in the day-to-day back office operations that they lose focus on their core products, services, and clients."

Jeff Rich, CEO, ACS, 2002.

The commercial marketplace has embraced BPO, which emerged as an extension of IT outsourcing. Under business process outsourcing a provider assumes responsibility for performing a specific business process, typically a technology-intensive, labor intensive, data intensive, or clerical or repetitive process. These processes lend themselves to operational solutions that scale – and thus become attractive business opportunities to corporate solution providers. Gartner projects that the size of BPO in all sectors will grow dramatically over the next few years, as organizations strive to improve their profitability (reduced costs, greater quality, and competitiveness) and their balance sheet performance (avoid investing capital in improving process performance). While higher education has lagged behind other industries in embracing business process outsourcing, that is likely to change over the next five years, in the face of financial exigency and the increasing capacity to deconstruct and reintegrate business processes using Web services.

The ECAR Survey forecast a CAGR at 14 percent for BPO between 2001 and 2006. One can readily see the drivers from a VOI perspective and the gains from a VOI perspective.

For the past several years, providers such as ACS, Collegis, Tuition Management Systems, BearingPoint, and other consulting and services firms have begun to offer resourcing services to higher education, dealing with selected processes. Where available, outsourcing can offer the following returns:

- Improve productivity and operational efficiencies
- Enhance service
- Reduce costs and capital requirements
- Focus energies on core businesses
- Ensure best practices, skills, and technologies
- Gain access to scalable operations and on-demand resources

Chapter 3 provides a review and discussion of several case studies that illustrate a number of state-of-the-art resourcing applications. The savings from successful outsourcing arrangements result from process improvement (through use of technology, centralization, and simplification), labor rate arbitrage, and economies of scale (achieved through shared services).

The potentials from BPO will increase as Web services enable the development of loosely coupled systems and processes. Loose coupling will make it easier to deconstruct and resource particular parts of business processes. In *E-Business in Education*, we characterized this as "surgical outsourcing." The case studies in Chapter 3, and the discussion in Chapter 4, explore the full implications of deconstructed, reinvented, loosely coupled business processes, all in the context of the new business value web framework.

Shared Services

Shared services refers to the practice of providing services and solutions, the components of which are to some extent shared with multiple participants. Shared services can take many forms.

Shared Services in Large, Multi-Site, or Global Organizations

Large corporate enterprises have increasingly used shared services centers to serve functions such as finance, human resources, procurement, and customer services. Over 60 percent of Fortune 500 companies had shared services centers by 2000. Many multi-campus institutions have utilized variations of shared service centers in their finance and human resources functions. Moreover, many institutions provide IT services in a shared services mode.

Collaborative Development Across Enterprises

Colleges and universities often band together to create a software application or service that is beyond the capacity of any single institution, to reduce the cost of such development, or to reach a broader audience. Consider the following examples:

- The Boston Consortium is a group of 13 institutions in the Boston area that are dedicated to reducing costs and increasing quality in higher education. They have created an enterprise network to develop the competencies and perspectives of staff in the institutions and to incubate pilot projects. The group has launched a shared services program in risk management that is jointly developed and managed by five participating institutions. Similar programs are under development. Chapter 3 contains a case study on The Boston Consortium.

- Many higher education systems have banded together to purchase jointly or to co-develop major IT platforms or application software suites. The California State University System has jointly acquired and customized an ERP platform. The University System of Georgia has acquired a Learning Management System

The Shared Services Delivery Model

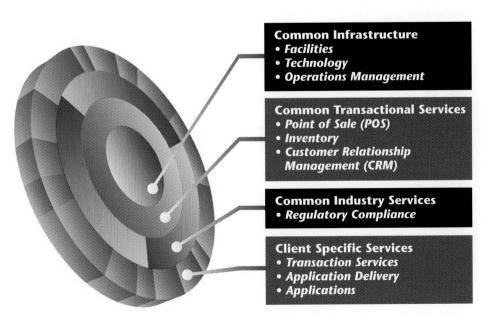

Common Infrastructure
- *Facilities*
- *Technology*
- *Operations Management*

Common Transactional Services
- *Point of Sale (POS)*
- *Inventory*
- *Customer Relationship Management (CRM)*

Common Industry Services
- *Regulatory Compliance*

Client Specific Services
- *Transaction Services*
- *Application Delivery*
- *Applications*

The shared services approaches span the many dimensions of business service infrastructures, from common infrastructure through service delivery operations and finally point solutions for individual clients of participating businesses.

"The cost is in the transaction. We must reduce the number and complexity of our transactions."

Robert Zemsky

for all campuses. Four institutions in Australia have jointly developed a digital asset management platform.

- The E&I Coop has made the HigherMarkets/Sciquest procurement platform available to members so that they can purchase the products being made available to cooperative members.

- George Mason University at Prince William County has partnered with the county to develop a recreational facility available to both campus and community users. This creative, public/private partnership utilized the combined financing/debt support of both parties.

These shared services examples, and others, are explored in greater detail in Chapter 3.

Use of Application Service Provider or Business Process Outsourcing Partner

Both application service providers and business process outsourcers rely on shared services to provide savings to their customers. The preferred mode of operation is to provide a common infrastructure (facilities, technology, and operations management), common transactional services, and common industry services (regulatory compliance), married with client specific services, including the preservation of proprietary and/or distinctive processes that yield competitive advantage. By leveraging common people, processes, and technology, these providers furnish world-class infrastructure without the capital outlay and cost structure required to maintain comparable in-house operations.

Process Reinvention

In the 1990s, enterprises in all business sectors, including education, engaged in business process reengineering, using the first generation of knowledge management tools and philosophies.

Outcomes of Process Reinvention

Most of these efforts were disappointing because they focused on simple gains in productivity through efficiency and failed to recognize the richness of tacit knowledge that employees held about how processes really worked. They failed to understand the real value of processes. The personnel reductions and reallocations of energies made by first-generation process reengineering efforts helped enterprises trim costs, but at the price of reduced effectiveness.

Today, we use *process reinvention* to describe the reinvention of business processes undertaken with a keen appreciation of value. New technologies enable staff to interact more effectively with other staff and customers; acquire, assimilate, and share knowledge dramatically more effectively; and personalize services so clients can serve themselves. As a result, institutions can deconstruct their current approaches to business processes and reinvent them.

The dividends are a combination of productivity enhancement and improved service and customer satisfaction. Process reinvention changes organizational dynamics and the nature of relationships with stakeholders. Process reinvention can occur in a number of ways.

Outsourcing to Reinvent Process

Many of the processes provided by BPOs can be considered "best practice" and are more efficient and effective than the institutional processes they are replacing. Even if elements of the institutional process are truly distinctive and a source of competitive advantage, they can be grafted into the BPO process to create a superior, reinvented process. A BPO relationship is an opportunity to achieve a reinvention of outsourced processes.

An example is the University of Phoenix, which engaged in financial aid outsourcing with Affiliated Computing Services (ACS) in 1999. We discuss this example in the case study discussions in Chapter 3.

Use ERP Tools to Enable Reinvention and Rethinking

Enterprise resource planning systems provide full information integration and workflow tools that enable institutional leadership to deconstruct and reinvent processes. The University of Delaware offers an example of a major process reinvention initiative that was tied to new technology capabilities and a new physical facility serving enrollment services functions. In the early 1990s, the university used the implementation of a new student information system to reinvent its enrollment services using a "one-stop shopping" model. An historic schoolhouse near the campus was converted to a Student Services Center, where students could go for any student services activity, from traffic tickets to course registration to student accounting. Most enrollment services staff were converted from specialists in admission, financial aid, student accounting, or registration, to generalists capable of answering most student needs in the full range of enrollment services functions. A small core of policy specialists was stationed in other administration offices to answer the small number of specialized questions that could not be answered by the student service generalists.

These changes altered the institution's culture of student service and simplified the process of student problem solving. Over the course of time, more and more students began to use the terminals in the Student Services Center to answer their own questions; then the campus network. This evolution resulted in "student no-stop shopping."

Business officers today should look to the purchase of an ERP with a view to ensure the minimization of customization. In this way, they implement the versions of institutional business processes embedded in the ERP solution, which have been refined through years of development and continuous improvement. By studying these processes as "best practice," institutional leaders reinvent their existing processes.

Today's process reinvention techniques seek to create flexible, loosely coupled prototypes that can be continuously evolved.

Principles of Process Reinvention

- *Use the integration and workflow tools in ERP solutions to reinvent processes*

- *Accept best practices embedded in BPO and ERP solutions*

- *Limit customization to processes where your institution's distinctive approach provides competitive advantage*

- *Use portal and Web services to deconstruct and stitch together processes in different ways and change how stakeholders experience products and services*

- *To the fullest extent possible, enable students, faculty, staff, and other stakeholders to solve their own problems rather than requiring intervention or assistance*

- *Actively evaluate the portfolio of processes for reinvention potential*

Deploy Enterprise Portals to Change How Stakeholders Experience Processes

Enterprise portals enable institutions to literally change how students, faculty, staff, donors, and other stakeholders "experience" the products, services, and knowledge available online. The University of Minnesota used the opportunity provided by its portal development to improve the quality and efficiency of student services, in the process turning students into personal problem solvers. This reinvention changed the dynamics of the service environment. Institutions as diverse as Florida Community College of Jacksonville, Johns Hopkins University, and MIT have utilized Web services to reinvent portalized services.

The next five years promise to yield new combinations of ERP, learning management system (LMS), learning content management system (LCMS), enterprise portal, e-portfolio, Web services, and other applications tools. Taken together, these will afford unparalleled opportunities for process reinvention, shared services, and business process outsourcing.

Resourcing to Optimize and Leverage Value

While resourcing deals with the issue of what relationships and approaches to utilize in creating a portfolio of business process solutions, it has a more profound goal: to optimize the *value* that business processes provide to the institution and its stakeholders.

Resourcing Optimizes Value

In a landmark article titled "After Reengineering Comes Resourcing" in the *NACUBO Business Officer*, (August 1998), Frederick J. Turk introduced the phrase "resourcing" to business and auxiliary affairs officers. Turk's approach called for institutional leadership to reflect on the *value* added by the institution's processes and to create new resource solutions to address these needs.

"Resourcing is an emerging concept that encourages leadership to think differently about how to accomplish a strategic vision by applying a portfolio decision process in identifying the core and noncore activities of the institution and by utilizing creative resource solutions to perform these activities."

Frederick J. Turk, 1998, p. 1.

In Turk's view, higher education has a 40-year history of using outsourcing to address functions such as bookstores and food services. Recently, outsourcing had been applied to a range of other functions. Moreover, some institutions had utilized reengineering to cut costs through changing administrative processes.

Frederick J. Turk is well-known for his expertise in outsourcing. He served as president of ARAMARK, Campus Services and as partner-in-charge of KPMG's higher education business and is currently on the board of Tuition Management Systems, a business process resourcer of tuition payment solutions.

Assessing Mission Criticality and Performance

Turk challenges leaders to assess their process portfolios with the dual lenses of mission criticality and performance.

Evaluating Candidates for Resourcing

Resourcing decisions are driven by a combination of mission criticality and performance of business processes.

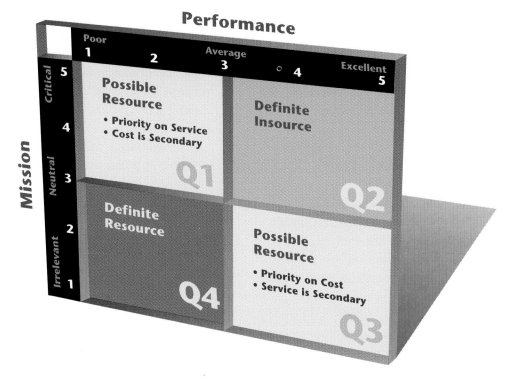

Leverage is achieved when existing assets are combined in new ways through innovation, or when internal and external assets and competencies are combined in ways that would not be possible with internal resources alone.

But resourcing provides the opportunity to move beyond outsourcing and process reinvention by developing new, broader relationships with outside enterprises. These new relationships enable an institution to establish competitive advantage and pursue its distinctive academic mission.

Turk suggested that institutional leadership continuously reflect on its portfolio of processes, services, and activities, using two lenses: 1) mission criticality of the activity, process, or service and 2) current level of performance. The matrix arrays a comparison of services/processes assessed using this technique.

• *Quadrant I* focuses on activities that are mission critical (score greater than "3" on a 1-5 scale) yet for which the current level of performance is less than average (less than a score of "3" on a 1-5 scale). Institutions cannot sustain competitive advantage if mission critical performance is average or less. So these cases are candidates for resourcing if partners can be found whose track record suggests

they can improve performance. For such cases, cost is secondary; the key is to improve performance of the service.

• *Quadrant II* portrays processes/activities whose mission criticality ranges from slightly above neutral to critical, and whose current performance scales go from above average to excellent. Such services are usually provided by the institution on an insource basis. Even insourced, high-performing services, however, are candidates for internal reinvention to enhance quality and/or reduce or control costs.

• *Quadrant III* focuses on less-than-critical services, for which performance is above average. These are candidates for possible resourcing, for which the priority is reduced cost. If a resourcing partner can be found who has a track record of delivering such services at a lower cost than currently experienced, at a satisfactory level of quality, items in this quadrant are strong resourcing candidates.

• *Quadrant IV* focuses on services with low mission criticality and poor cost performance. These are strong candidates for resourcing and related reinvention.

In reality, this matrix is only a rough guide to be customized by individual institutions. Some institutions may set different breakpoints for where service is considered mission critical and when resourcing is considered.

Since Turk developed this matrix, a number of conditions have changed. Institutions have developed more experience with a wide range of outsourcing opportunities and providers. They have also acquired experience with moving from insource to outsource and back again, using resourcing partners to build institutional sophistication

and competencies. Further, the capacities of enterprises providing solution support and services have expanded and diversified to include both broad business process outsourcing (BPO) and "point" solutions in targeted services. The use of Web-based services and interactivity has accelerated the development of resourcing solutions using these tools.

"An important part of resourcing the enterprise involves taking some time to step back and periodically assess whether functions and activities are creating value. This is especially true as a leadership applies resourcing techniques in assessing how functions can be most effective and efficient in supporting institutional mission."

Frederick J. Turk, 1998, p. 4.

Leverage creates a value explosion producing tremendous advantage to the institution.

Evaluating Candidates for Resourcing

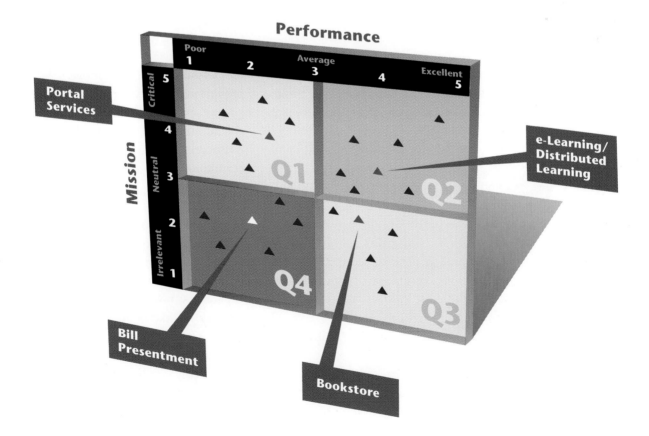

Optimizing Value for a Portfolio of Processes, Services, and Activities

Resourcing is about more than making insource/outsource decisions. It involves managing and leveraging the institution's portfolio of process, services, and activities so as to optimize value. Consider the following examples.

A certain formula for optimizing value is to focus on the needs of students. Resourcing partners need to be fully committed to the institutional mission of service to students.

In *Quadrant I*, portal services is highlighted as an example. It is inherently mission critical but is currently being performed poorly. As such, it is a strong candidate for resourcing through outsourcing, technology partnership, consulting arrangements, or some combination. But the issue is not just how should the portal service be developed and provided, but how the portal drives value for the institution. The resourcing decision should include setting aggressive goals for driving value through the enterprise portal.

Process and services falling in *Quadrant II* are both mission critical and well performed, so they should likely remain insourced. The example we have chosen is e-learning/ distributed learning, which is currently insourced in this example. Yet such processes/services are likely not living up to their full value potential, given the potential

of portal services to stimulate process reinvention and create new experiences for students, faculty staff, donors, and other stakeholders. The different processes in the portfolio are interconnected, and decisions for one process affect others.

Quadrant III holds processes, services, and activities that are well performed, but are not mission critical. Such services are candidates for outsourcing. For example, the bookstore or food services operation at a public university may be performing fairly well but still be a candidate for outsourcing, where the outsourcing arrangement can result in cost savings and freeing up of management energy to focus on other issues. But the value assessment should proceed beyond the choice of resourcing vendors and relationships to assure that the service is being full leveraged to maximize its value contribution to the institution. For example, are the roles of the bookstore in e-business, e-learning, knowledge asset management being fully leveraged?

Quadrant IV contains low mission criticality services that are not performing well. Such processes/services are strong candidates for full outsourcing. Take, for example, bill presentment. If its performance today is poor, it should definitely be outsourced. It should not only be evaluated for outsourcing, but also in terms of its value contribution and relationship to other services.

Business officers have been helping their institutional leadership deal with issues of value for some time. But the advent of Web-based processes, services, and experiences has raised the stakes and created new dimensions to the question of value. The business, auxiliary, and administrative services office is emerging as the key player in the cross-functional teams that are evaluating an institution's portfolio of processes for continuous improvement and value enhancement.

CHAPTER 2

Getting Value from Business Processes and Solutions

- *Changing Sources of Value for 21st Century Enterprises*
- *Evolving From ROI to VOI*
- *Examples of VOI in Higher Education*
- *Using VOI to Respond to Tough Times, Big Choices*

Enterprises of all kinds – colleges and universities, corporations, associations, government agencies, and other non-profits – are discovering new sources of value in the Knowledge Economy. They are also inventing new strategies for unleashing these sources of value to enhance their products, services and experiences and to establish competitive advantage. The value embedded in an enterprise's assets is like the potential energy in a spring, waiting to be released. Leveraging the value embedded in an enterprise's assets has become the new driver of growth in the Knowledge Economy.

The traditional approach has been to measure the tangible sources of value through return on investment (ROI). But many of the intangible returns from technology create so-called "soft" outcomes that are not captured by ROI. A new concept, value on investment (VOI) is presented that harvests the impact of the value created by process reinvention, leveraging knowledge assets, collaboration, creating communities of reflective practice, building individual and enterprise competencies, and enabling new kinds and levels of leadership.

Return and value are inextricably interconnected. Gains in value today often result in greater returns tomorrow. The intangible outcomes comprising value can stimulate tangible returns over time.

VOI is experienced along three dimensions in colleges and universities. Scope of initiative ranges from tactical/incremental to strategic. Organizational impact can include individual performance, enterprise-wide performance (competitive parity), and strategic direction (competitive advantage). Organization dynamics ranges from productivity to collaboration, to innovation, the greatest source of value. Examples are provided of how these sources of value have been generated in higher education.

Business officers are uniquely positioned to guide their institutions in understanding the value embedded in processes, services, and strategies.

Terms and Concepts

Accountability: This refers to holding colleges and universities accountable for their performance and outcomes. Over the next few years, pressures for accountability will continue to increase.

Collaboration: This involves working together to develop solutions, discover new best practices, and build competencies. Collaboration is necessary to accelerate and maximize innovation.

Competitive Parity: Actions that imitate other institutions produce competitive parity, rather than advantage.

Innovation: Transforming the dynamics of organizational processes, through innovation, is a key source of business value and competitive advantage.

Leveraging Value Assets: Enterprises build synergy and competitive advantage through leveraging their assets.

Performance Measurement: Over the next several years, colleges and universities will be required to maintain far more sophisticated performance and accountability measures. New GASB/FASB regulations and state performance standards will drive this development.

Productivity: This is the ability of individuals and teams to create a quantity of output of a certain quality.

Return on Investment: ROI is a measurement of the tangible benefits of a technology investment. The "R" in ROI is based on measurable cost savings and enhancements in productivity. ROI typically speaks to tactical assets of the institution.

Transparency: Clarity of financial reporting and performance management reporting will be critical to government and university stakeholders.

Value: Value is the benefit derived from an enterprise's assets by its stakeholders. Business processes are the gateways through which stakeholders experience the institution's assets. Processes add value to those engaged in them. In colleges and universities, value is achieved by participation in the full range of academic and administrative processes and services.

Value Chain: This is a sequential chain of activities and relationships that adds value to business processes. E-Knowledge enables the unbundling and reinvention of traditional value chains for learning and knowledge management and the enterprise activities that depend on them. The traditional value chain becomes a value web in tomorrow's e-knowledge environment.

Value on Investment: VOI goes a step beyond ROI to assess the intangibles that may result from an institutional technology investment. The "V" in VOI consists of: 1) capacity to reinvent business processes, 2) enhancement of knowledge asset management, 3) greater capacity to collaborate and form/participate in communities of practice, 4) enhanced individual and enterprise competencies, and 5) support of new leadership. VOI is based on changes in the dynamics of the institution that enable greater collaboration and innovation and is linked to mission and vision. VOI addresses aspects of the strategic assets of the institution.

Value Web or Value Net: The simple, linear value chain has become a multi-dimensional value net or a value web. Institutions can build solutions using a variety of resources and services, both internal and external, from a variety of solution providers. The resulting **business value net** or **business value web** is multi-dimensional.

Changing Sources of Value for 21st Century Enterprises

Across the Knowledge Economy, enterprises of all kinds are evolving new notions of what creates value for 21st century organizations. They are embracing the importance of "soft" or "intangible" initiatives/outcomes, rather than the "hard" and "tangible" measures that are reflected in traditional measures such as ROI. The potential transformative power of collaboration, innovation, knowledge management, business process reinvention, communities of practice, and productivity enhancement are becoming widely recognized as essential determinants of value and competitiveness for Knowledge Age enterprises.

Gartner (2001) opined that in the late 20th century, only the most progressive enterprises comprehended the importance of such intangibles. By 2006, Gartner predicted, "50 percent of Fortune 1000 companies will identify an owner for workplace initiatives, formally track and manage intangible assets, and measure investment vs. value creation." (Gartner, 2001, p.1) Gartner introduced the concept of *VOI* both to measure such developments and to hold enterprises to a higher standard of performance/aspiration from their investments in information and communications technology (ICT). Gartner's conceptual framework included the five elements of VOI, the three dimensions of VOI, and the graphic represented on page 21.

"VOI is key to understanding the real strategic pay-offs from technology to enterprises over the next decade."

Donald Norris, Jon Mason, and Paul Lefrere, Transforming e-Knowledge, *p. 105.*

The potential importance of VOI was further illustrated in *Transforming e-Knowledge: A Revolution in the Sharing of Knowledge* (Norris, Mason, and Lefrere, 2003), which asserted that successful Knowledge Age enterprises will need to dramatically enhance the capacity of individuals and organizations to acquire, assimilate, and share knowledge. To achieve such an order-of-magnitude leap in capabilities will require not only new infrastructures and reinvented processes, but also fundamental changes in the knowledge culture of organizations of all kinds. VOI is the benchmark of this transformation, serving two purposes: 1) a standard for measuring the tangible and intangible returns from investing in technology, and 2) a stretch goal that encourages enterprises to leverage technology investments to change organizational dynamics so as to create new sources of value that will be the new gold standard for the Knowledge Age.

The current economic doldrums are causing many enterprises both to seek new sources of competitive advantage and to reduce the costs/enhance the productivity of their current operations. Higher education has been especially hard hit. Over the next few years, institutions will need to make tough choices and big ones if they are to cope with threats and take advantage of opportunities. The effective use of information and communication technology will be an important instrument of cost reduction/productivity enhancement as well as means of transforming processes and practices and organizational dynamics to achieve new levels of performance. Put simply, institutions may not be able to justify investment in technology if they are not willing to transform their practices, processes, and organizational dynamics, as measured by VOI. In this context, their value dimension is both a benchmark and a call to action.

"When a new model changes the economics of an industry and is difficult to replicate, it can by itself create a strong competitive advantage."

Joan Magretta

Competitive Advantage:
Institutions that are differentiated from their competitors, and seen as creating greater value for stakeholders, experience competitive advantage. Innovation, a key element of VOI, generates competitive advantage.

Evolving From ROI to VOI

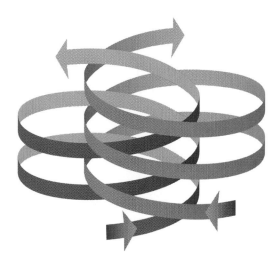

ROI and VOI are inextricably linked. Over time, increases in value create increases in return, sometimes directly, often indirectly. Return and value are like two interconnected springs, each reinforcing the other. Freeing the springs releases the latent energy contained within.

The differences between return on investment and value on investment are simple. ROI is based on "return," which is generated by tangible, traditional outcomes such as conventional enhancement of productivity or cost reduction, enhanced revenues, and opening of new markets. ROI focuses on traditional measures. ROI is objective, based on concrete measures, although the assumptions driving ROI may be subjective and judgmental.

VOI is the measure of the total value of "soft" or "intangible" benefits derived from technology initiatives. ROI is part of VOI. "Value" is generated through outcomes that enhance productivity, build collaboration, and enable innovation. Value-building initiatives change the organization's dynamics through the following elements:

- Supporting business process reinvention and innovation;
- Enabling collaboration and increasing capabilities to learn and develop communities;
- Formalizing the cultivation, management, and leveraging of knowledge assets;
- Increasing individual and organizational competencies; and
- Enabling new kinds and levels of leadership.

Measurement of VOI uses nontraditional measures, in combination with the traditional measures of ROI. VOI is subjective and judgmental. It is also contextual, depending on the perspective and position of the evaluating party – trustees, presidents, provosts, CFOs, CIOs, other vice presidents, managers, or stewards of organizational processes. VOI links to the vision and mission of the enterprise and reflects the strategic worth of the asset in context.

Dimensions of VOI

In addition to describing VOI through these five elements, Gartner suggests three critical dimensions of VOI: 1) scope of initiative, 2) organizational impact, and 3) organizational dynamics. The graphic on the next page portrays these three dimensions as axes.

Scope of Initiative (Horizontal Axis). Initiatives can range from tactical to strategic in scope. *Tactical* initiatives tend to be operational in impact, improving the efficiency of the current operating environment and generating incremental value. They can also apply to only a portion of the enterprise. *Strategic* initiatives focus on broadly increasing the effectiveness of the current environment and/or inventing capabilities for the future environment; they intentionally aim for transformative results spanning the entire enterprise.

Organizational Impact (Vertical Axis). This dimension captures the intentionality of the initiative. Impacts can range from those that affect individual performance to enterprise performance/competitiveness to impacts that affect strategic direction/ competitive advantage. If the organizational impact is on *individual performance*, VOI tends to be tactical in nature and value lies in the

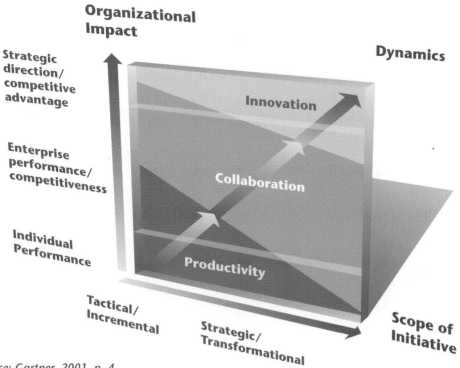

VOI is shaped by three dimensions: scope of the initiative, organizational impact, and dynamics.

Source: Gartner, 2001, p. 4.

improvement of personal job performance. While some strategic impact will result from the uncoordinated efforts of individuals, such results will be uneven. ***Enterprise performance*** initiatives are designed to have an impact at a higher level and can produce a combination of strategic and tactical VOI. These initiatives target large groups and can create competitive parity. ***Strategic direction*** initiatives begin with the intention of providing VOI that is strategic and transformative. They generate value by achieving the vision embodied in the institution's strategic direction, and they push beyond mere parity to genuine competitive advantage.

Dynamics (Diagonal Axis). Value is driven primarily by changes in organizational dynamics. Changing the dynamics of the organization can range from enhancing productivity to collaboration to innovation. As the scope of the initiatives grows from tactical to strategic, and as the organizational impact grows from affecting individual performance to achieving strategic advantage, the dynamics of VOI range from enhancing productivity, to

producing collaboration, to inspiring innovation. As VOI dynamics expand, the magnitude of the value-creating energy released increases exponentially, rather than linearly. ***Productivity*** is about greater efficiency, doing more with less. ***Collaboration*** integrates quantity and quality, outcomes and deliverables. Collaboration is the bridge between productivity and innovation. ***Innovation*** has the highest value-creating capacity because it reveals new ways of doing old things and new experiences that create competitive advantage. Innovation in organizational dynamics redefines products, services, relationships, and experiences.

Gartner identifies innovation as the key element in value creation for Knowledge Age enterprises. They predict that by 2004, 25 percent of enterprises will actively manage innovation as a core business process (0.6 probability), which will create competitive advantage. In Gartner's view, most enterprises treat "soft" initiatives as long-term, but not strategic investments. This should change as enterprises actively manage and measure VOI.

Examples of VOI in Higher Education

Reinventing and innovating business processes will be the centerpiece of VOI for most institutions. Many colleges and universities need to develop greater skill at innovation rather than imitation.

Most institutional initiatives affect a number of the elements of value, at the same time. In order to understand how VOI looks in higher education, we will focus on each of the five elements of VOI, selecting examples that demonstrate each of the elements in different combinations of the three dimensions of VOI.

Reinvent Business Processes and Innovate

Colleges and universities have used the opportunity provided by new technology to reinvent business processes. Few have taken full advantage of these opportunities, however. In recent years, the primary focus of process reinvention has been seen in using ERP, LCMS, portals, and other elements of the ICT infrastructure to reinvent business processes, the dynamics of interactions with stakeholders, and other aspects of institutional culture.

Tactical Scope/ Individual Performance/ Productivity. Pioneering ERP implementations used modified/customized ERP to memorialize existing institutional

processes. Even if they talked strategically, these early implementations acted tactically and focused on individual productivity. Not only were such approaches costly, but they also failed to reinvent institutional processes or achieve significant innovation in relationships and services. In fact, too often these efforts had the effect of "hard wiring" existing processes against loosely coupled revised processes. Some positive ROI was achieved through enhancement of individual performance and productivity, but little strategic value resulted. Even today, many institutions implementing ERP focus on individual productivity and fail to use process reinvention to change the dynamics of the institution's interactions with stakeholders. ECAR's Research Study, *The Promise and Performance of Enterprise Systems for Higher Education*, suggests that few institutions have used ERP as a platform for process reinvention.

Tactical-Strategic Scope/ Enterprise Performance/ Collaboration. The workflow tools, integrated information flows, and community-building capabilities in state-of-the-art ERP systems and solutions enable institutions to facilitate collaboration among and between groups and communities of faculty and administrative staff. Web site and portal development enable communication with all the institution's publics, both internal and external. Even without extensive process reinvention, the level and speed of transaction processing and the quality of customer service can improve to parity with the level of other institutions. Many institutions today are moving into this area of VOI.

Strategic Scope/ Strategic Direction/ Innovation. The implementation of state-of-the-art ERP provides an unprecedented opportunity to accept the best practices imbedded in the solution provider's software and to reinvent institutional processes and

Support Business Process Reinvention

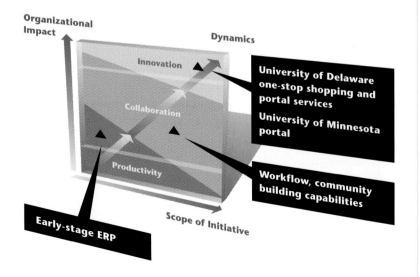

dynamics. This is facilitated by the use of the enterprise portal to reshape how students, faculty, staff, alumni, donors, and stakeholders experience learning, other services, processes, and knowledge. The combinations of these activities can create not just competitive parity, but also competitive advantage. Leading-edge institutions are focusing on strategic innovation through continuous process improvement and creating new experiences for stakeholders. This cycle of process reinvention begins with the implementation of the ERP and continues over six or seven years as staff understand the potentials for changing the dynamics of processes and practices through collaboration and innovation.

Ten years ago, leading-edge institutions such as the University of Delaware used earlier stage ERP systems as a foundation for reinventing their enrollment services functions to create "one-stop shopping" for students and to turn most enrollment service professionals into generalists, with a few policy specialists. Over time, students were encouraged to solve their own problems using online support services. Recent developments in portalized services have enabled the University of Delaware to advance even further. Similarly, the University of Minnesota's portal initiative led to substantial changes in institutional policies, simplification of the process challenges facing students, and enabling of students to solve their own problems. These innovations are significantly changing institutional dynamics.

"Portals, integrated into backend campus administrative systems, have the potential to significantly reduce the cost and raise the quality of campus services."

David Hollowell,
www.udel.edu/ExecVP/onestop,
February 2003.

What kinds of innovation are possible through portal and ERP-enabled process reinvention? Richard Katz and Robert Kvavik (2002) emphasize using portalized, reinvented processes to free students, faculty, and staff from "administrivia" and customer unfriendly processes. Self-service, convenient and easy service, and transparency of rules and regulations are all elements that future stakeholders will demand of our campus environments.

The dynamics of campus processes must also facilitate the fusion of learning, research, public service, personal life management, recreation, and civic affairs, all through the campus portal, the gateway to the "experience layer" through which students, faculty, staff, and other stakeholders engage the products, services, experiences, and knowledge that colleges and universities offer. As Carl Berger points out (2002), this is the ultimate killer application for 21st century colleges and universities, and it will result from expeditionary, innovative reinvention of basic campus business processes.

Collaborate and Enhance the Capacity to Develop Communities

Collaboration is key to building competencies, enhancing innovation, and maximizing VOI. It is the bridge between simple productivity enhancement and innovation. Moreover, communities of practice are likely to be the dominant organizational form of the 21st century enterprise. Today's colleges and universities have both informal and formal communities of practice in place. They await the stimulus of enterprise-wide commitment and innovation to substantially enhance and release the value in enterprise business processes and practices.

Tactical Scope/Individual Performance/ Productivity. Pioneering ERP and campus e-mail provided communication tools and

"When done well, the portal can approach the mythical 90/8/2 customer service model:
- *90 percent of user transactions are conducted in a self-service mode*
- *8 percent of user transactions are provided with a combination of self-service and user support staff help*
- *2 percent of user transactions receive the high quality support of face-to-face staff help"*

David Hollowell

Enabling collaboration and enhancing the capacity to develop communities of practice is a strong potential contributor to VOI, extending and enhancing the impacts of process reinvention and innovation.

Formalizing the management of knowledge and intellectual assets is an area of substantial potential for enhancing VOI for colleges and universities. It is also an area in which most institutions are at a relatively elementary level of development.

transaction-oriented processing that let individuals collaborate more effectively with others on campus, around job/project-related issues and building personal productivity. These capabilities enabled the development of informal communities of practice, or the enhancement of existing social networks related to faculty, academic support, and administrative services. Without a conscious commitment to enterprise-wide collaboration and communities of practice, the VOI from such initiatives remained low.

Tactical-Strategic Scope/Enterprise Performance/Collaboration. Formal communities of practice have been created in several ways: 1) ERP and other large-scale technology projects created communities that featured online project resources, help desks, project teams organized by functional/technical interests and responsibilities, and both formal and informal patterns of interaction through e-mail and meetings. 2) These implementation communities eventually migrated into solution provider user groups. 3) CMS/LMS solution providers created both on-campus communities on e-learning practices and cross-institutional user groups focusing on best practices.

4) Administrative applications such as e-procurement formed internal communities of purchasers (both central purchasing professionals and departmental staff engaged in purchasing) and cross-institutional user groups. 5) Other administrative and academic support communities in enrollment services, counseling, and other student services have been formed to provide one-stop shopping and other services.

Strategic Scope/ Strategic Direction/ Innovation. After learning how to use communities of practice for collaboration, leading-edge institutions have built on these early-stage communities to innovate and to serve the enterprise's strategic direction through providing better service to stakeholders. In e-learning, the communities of practice advance institutional practice through sharing best practices and participating in e-knowledge repositories and marketplaces. In academic support and administrative services, cross-institutional communities of practice enable institutions to adapt best practices from other settings and to involve faculty, staff, students, and other stakeholders in feedback and reinvention of processes and relationships. At this stage, these communities of practice advance the process of continuous reinvention, raising it to higher levels of achievement.

Communities of practice serve several purposes. First, they involve the grassroots in problem solving and decision making. Second, they spread information and knowledge on processes and practices so that they are available to everyone. This access to information is empowering.

"The information-based organization and the infrastructure supporting it enable an institution to liberate the members of the institutional community from the tyranny and oppression of institutional rules, processes, and administrivia."

Richard Katz, 2002.

Enhance Collaboration and Community Development

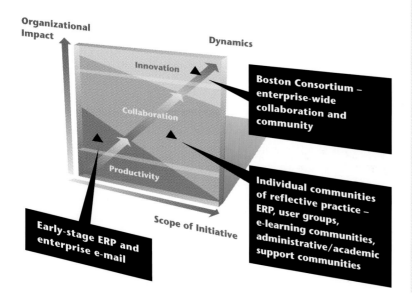

The Boston Consortium is a group of 13 private institutions formed by the chief financial officers of those institutions who serve as its board of directors. They are on the developmental path toward creating enterprise-wide collaborative environments dedicated to the development of individual, team, and institutional capacities, using collaboration to create innovative solutions applied to a wide range of administrative and academic support services. The consortium uses working groups to launch feasibility studies for hard-nosed initiatives that are designed to improve the quality of the academic/administrative experience and services for students, faculty, staff, and other stakeholders, all at a reduced cost. The consortium has created many useful solutions, including a shared services approach to risk management, with internal audit and legal affairs solutions under development. Technology is a key element in The Boston Consortium's solutions and in the efforts of other exemplary consortia to share products and services. Examples of other collaborative sharing include Kentucky Virtual University (academic tools and services), Ohio Learning Network (student services), Southern Regional Electronic College (multi-state access to electronic courses), and NextEd (international marketing of learning offerings), to name a few. New approaches to collaboration are also reflected in the emerging generation of institutional business solutions that are utilizing not just outsourcing but also resourcing of business solutions using a blend of internal and external expertise.

Cultivate, Manage, and Leverage Knowledge and Intellectual Assets

College and universities are knowledge-centered enterprises. Yet they take a "cottage industry" approach to the creation and sharing of knowledge. Recently, learning management systems and knowledge/content management

Cultivate, Manage, and Leverage Knowledge Assets

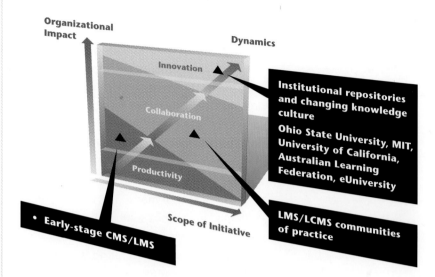

capabilities have become the primary focal points of institutional initiatives to make more strategic use of knowledge assets.

Tactical Scope/ Individual Performance/ Productivity. The first course management systems (CMS) and learning management systems (LMS) enabled institutions to digitize and "Webify" courses, creating both virtual and "blended" learning combining physical and virtual resources and experiences. Individual faculty developed the capacity to "move their courses online," and in the process they began to understand how to change their offerings to take better advantage of the Web. Over time, LMS vendors worked with institutions to create embryonic online repositories of these materials for the courses that have been moved online. This level of development produces incremental improvement and enhances the performance of individual faculty. It also provides insights into what will be needed to make further leaps in providing new, blended learning experiences for students. On most campuses, however, less than half the faculty participates in e-learning at this stage of development.

Tactical-Strategic Scope/Enterprise Performance/Collaboration. Over time, more and more faculty are drawn into participation

LMS/LCMS: Learning Management Systems support online and blended learning. Learning Content Management Systems (LCMS) provide substantially more robust content management capabilities designed to support the creation, storage, assembly, and delivery of modular, reusable learning content.

Increasing individual and organizational competencies is one of higher education's greatest challenges. It is also a strong potential source of VOI from investments in technology that enable capability development. These enterprise and individual competencies are essential to realize VOI from knowledge management and process reinvention.

in blended learning. LMS solution providers create communities of practice enabling faculty to learn best practices from one another. These communities of practice span institutional boundaries through online communities and user groups run by solution providers. At this stage, enterprise-wide sharing of best practices leverages the contributions of groups of individual faculty. The percentage of faculty participating in blended learning on particular campuses approaches critical mass. The course content contained in campus solution provider repositories begins to be shared across campus boundaries, illustrating the potentials in knowledge sharing.

Strategic Scope/ Strategic Direction/ Innovation. Awakened to the potential of cross-institutional knowledge sharing, campuses build on their experiences with LMS/LCMS to complete the policies, protocols, and infrastructures needed for digital rights/asset management and knowledge asset management. Institutional repositories of learning objects, research materials, and contributions to refereed journals are created. Leading-edge institutions participate in cross-institutional knowledge sharing and in digital content marketplaces. The sharing of knowledge is

used to change the use of knowledge to support learning and the infusion of just-in-time-knowledge into learning processes at all levels. Institutions participating in this way are able to reap decisive advantages in the cost of content and in the quality of the learning experience.

Digital asset management (DAM) is receiving attention from many institutions. Leading institutions are creating knowledge repositories and/or superarchives (Ohio State University, MIT Dspace, and the University of California System Scholarship Repository, for example). Cross-enterprise efforts are popping up all over the world (MERLOT, the Learning Object Network, the Australian Le@rning Federation, and eUniversity in the United Kingdom). Initiatives such as the Open Knowledge Initiative (OKI) and the Open Courseware Initiative (OCW) are tapping into latent support for an open source approach to e-knowledge and e-learning. Taken together, these approaches herald the development of genuine marketplaces for e-content and create the context for the emergence of "e-knowledge commerce" to exchange e-knowledge, some for free and some for fee.

Increase Individual and Organizational Competencies

Competency development is essential to the enhancement of institutional culture that supports next generation e-learning, knowledge management, and personalized service to stakeholders, providing "what I need, when I need it." Competencies are equally necessary in administrative and academic support and in a customer service orientation.

Tactical Scope/ Individual Performance/ Productivity. Early stage development in e-learning and knowledge management focused on individuals acquiring competencies in Webifying learning. Over time, institutions built a critical mass of

Increase Individual and Organizational Competencies

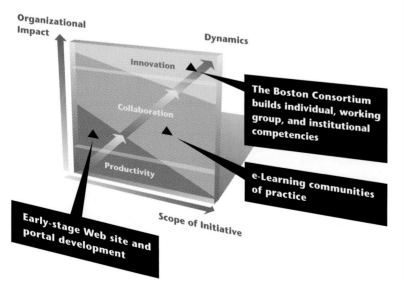

faculty with these competencies so they could learn from one another. Service to stakeholders also was treated in the early stages as a matter of individual development within existing academic support and administrative offices.

Tactical-Strategic Scope/ Enterprise Performance/ Collaboration. As institutions have developed Web site and portal capabilities, they have used them to personalize, reinvent, and enhance stakeholder services. At this stage of development, institutions have treated stakeholder service as an enterprise-wide effort, requiring new competencies and collaboration across the institution. On the e-learning and knowledge management front, institutions have used their communities of practice to develop e-learning knowledge-sharing infrastructures. Individual competencies are developed across the enterprise, but only for faculty who choose to participate.

Strategic Scope/ Strategic Direction/ Innovation. Leading-edge institutions with advanced portal developments have created individual and enterprise-wide competencies in enhancing service and devising new experiences for stakeholders of all kinds. These new experiences include all permutations of academic and administrative support. Enterprise competencies for supporting e-learning and knowledge management are further developed to create new learning and professional development experiences for learners and for faculty and researchers. As these infrastructures and capabilities are extended to include knowledge sharing in research, professional development, and e-learning, virtually all faculty and researchers will seek to participate.

Developing individual and organizational competencies is a substantial human resources challenge for institutions of higher education. The Boston Consortium is a

pioneering example. It is engaging faculty, staff, students, and suppliers in developing new competencies and patterns of behavior through innovation.

Achieve New Levels and Forms of Leadership

Leadership is needed to develop the infrastructures, applications, culture, solutions, and initiatives that yield significant VOI.

Tactical Scope/ Individual Performance/ Productivity. Individual productivity of leaders is enhanced by communication and interactivity tools that enable easier access to information.

Tactical-Strategic Scope/ Enterprise Performance/ Collaboration. Technology decisions have been driven up the organization chart. Moreover, most technology decisions are cross-cutting, requiring collaboration between many campus-level administrators and diverse user groups (see chart on page 90). Most decisions today have a technological element or implications. Enhanced collaboration in technology decision-making and process reinvention is a key source of VOI.

Achieving new levels and forms of leadership is essential to achieving breakthroughs in the resourcing of business processes and solutions in higher education. New approaches are necessary to nurture and unleash grassroots leadership skills.

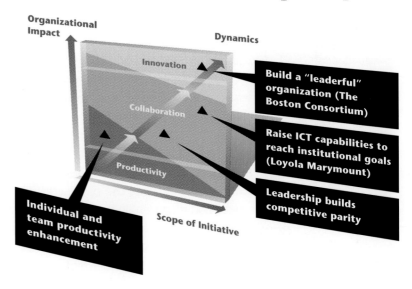

Leadership Development

VOI challenges institutions to raise their aspirations and use investments in technology and human resources to dramatically enhance value and build competitive advantage. It also provides benchmarks and metrics for assessing progress toward those goals.

"Over time, this value is increasingly the source of competitiveness, including increased value of brand, new and deeper core competencies, innovation, knowledge creation, increased depth and range of talent, and improved strength and diversity of human and technology networks. [Calculating VOI] requires full attention to the planning, design, funding, execution, and measurement of results."

Gartner Group, "Changing the View of ROI to VOI," Gartner Research Note on Strategic Planning, SPA-14-7250, p. 2.

It is supported by the workflow, knowledge-sharing, community, and interactivity capabilities provided by enhanced network and application infrastructures. Effective collaboration adds significant VOI, in the process establishing competitive parity.

Collaboration will enable institutions to eliminate unnecessary duplication in infrastructure and application platforms. Many institutions will agree on a single LMS or LCMS, and on interoperable solutions platforms. Collaborative, integrated solutions such as the SCT/WebCT/Campus Pipeline combination will be seen as important capabilities.

Strategic Scope/ Strategic Direction/ Innovation. For many institutions, competitive parity with a group of peer institutions is good enough – and a step forward from where they are today. Peer institutions and aspiration targets do not sit still, however, so leadership must learn how to leapfrog beyond competitive parity at today's standards to a higher plane. Leadership that advances the institution's strategic direction, through establishing distinctive advantage, is an even greater source of value. More and more, distinctiveness will be established through the Web site and portal experience, which is the university's brand image in the Knowledge Age.

The Boston Consortium, explored in the case studies in Chapter 3, offers an excellent example of building competitive advantage through leadership. It aims to establish a "leaderful environment" where grassroots leaders are developed and emerge at all levels.

Institutional leaders must comprehend and continuously articulate the ever-increasing expectation of stakeholders – students, faculty, staff, alumni, suppliers, and others. They must focus institutional innovation on the nature of the stakeholder experience.

This is especially critical considering that many experiences are co-created by participants.

ICT enables three distinct foci of strategic, institutional leadership that:
- Enhances Communication, Collaboration, and Community
- Facilitates Process Reinvention
- Opens New Revenue Potentials

An example of how technology enables a new level of leadership is seen at Loyola Marymount University. In order to achieve its strategic goal of becoming the leading Catholic university in the West, LMU needed to make a quantum leap in the quality and capacity of its ICT support. Through an enterprise-wide resourcing relationship with Collegis, Loyola Marymount is on track to achieve these objectives. The case studies in Chapter 3 outline this experience.

Conclusion: VOI Will Both Measure Outcomes and Stimulate Investment

Over the next decade, we believe VOI will become a primary benchmark against which investments in technology are gauged. The emerging standard will be to use technology investment to generate value that enhances the institution's competitive standing. Even conservative institutions such as colleges and universities will find it difficult to avoid making technology investments to protect their competitive standing. They will find it impossible to justify such investments without commitment to linking technology investment to process reinvention and measuring VOI.

Using VOI to Respond to Tough Times, Big Choices

Higher education has been hit, all at once, by an unusual combination of new challenges and opportunities:

- Declining economic conditions that affect public and personal finances
- A flood of red ink that drives cutbacks and tough decisions
- Increasing enrollments and demands for new services for students
- Demands for greater accountability and use of technology to expand access and reduce costs
- New opportunities, new markets, and new competitors

Institutional leaders are finding that traditional, piecemeal solutions are inadequate given the magnitude of today's challenges. Successful, new strategies and solutions have not yet emerged. The problem is as much developmental as strategic and programmatic. Even if the right solutions were more obvious than they are, they would prove difficult to implement, given the experience and capacity of institutional leadership. Campus management teams need to develop new capacities to craft solutions and to engage grassroots leadership in winning support for substantial change, both on and off campus.

Tough Times, Big Choices

Put simply, higher education needs to discover how to respond to tough times with not just tough choices, but big choices that will:

- develop the capacity of institutional leadership to mobilize support behind comprehensive, transformative initiatives that leverage institutional assets
- overcome traditional barriers to dramatic change, both internal and external

- reinvent current revenue streams and discover new ones
- reinvent programs, services, offerings, processes, and relationships
- use technology to reduce costs, reach new markets, and enhance relationships

To support this need for comprehensive reinvention of revenues and programs and leveraging of knowledge assets, we need new kinds of leadership that can change the organizational dynamics of higher education, set strategic direction, and aim for competitive excellence, not just parity. Greater collaboration and new competencies are needed, both individual and organizational. VOI is both the instrument for focusing attention on these issues and the means to achieve them.

VOI is not a blank check to invest more and more resources in ICT. Instead, it is the instrument for focusing attention on which results really matter and providing for their measurement.

Tough times, big choices require immediate action that will launch long-term, developmental initiatives. Such efforts aim to propel institutions on a new trajectory toward success.

Many institutions have lavished investment on technology and are puzzling over the return on that investment. VOI raises the stakes by focusing on the need to reinvent and transform processes to justify investment during tough financial times.

The value dimension can play an essential role in illuminating alternatives in at least three essential decision processes facing institutions. In each of these processes, VOI "raises the bar" for institutional aspirations to enhance value and provides methods and metrics to assess progress and adjust performance.

• VOI can shape the development of enterprise technology and human resources infrastructures, focusing on the need for commitment to transformative change, not just greater productivity. The value dimension should be used to set targets and stretch goals for ERP, LMS/LCMS, and portal decisions and for investing in human resources development.

• Second, VOI can be an essential element in resourcing the institution's business process portfolio and creating innovative solutions. VOI can guide the resourcing decision, setting of targets, and monitoring of performance for each process. Such continuous reinvention is key to ongoing institutional value building.

• Third, VOI can inspire and guide the efforts of institutions to craft strategic responses to the mixture of challenges and opportunities – tough times, big choices – that currently confront higher education. VOI can be used to establish stretch goals that reach beyond competitive parity to competitive advantage.

To date, most institutions have tinkered with the dynamics of organizational processes, achieving moderate ROI and modest VOI from investments in technology and human resources infrastructures. However, the case studies in Chapter 3 have identified institutions that may be on the threshold of truly significant VOI breakthroughs.

Key Questions About VOI

Leadership in higher education can use a combination of ROI and VOI to raise the stakes in using information and communications technology and human resource development to change the dynamics of institutional processes, services, and experiences. Several key questions emerge:

• How do we operationalize VOI in dealing with infrastructure development, resourcing business processes, and strategically responding to big choices in tough times?

• What can be learned from the case studies that describe the value generated by process reinvention, leveraging knowledge assets, and other elements of VOI?

• Is VOI the responsibility of senior leadership and ROI the responsibility of grassroots staff, or are responsibilities shared? How can we raise the understanding of value among grassroots staff and faculty? Other leaders?

• Can we learn any lessons from other industries that place greater stock than does higher education on innovation and competitive advantage? How are they measuring the value from innovation, collaboration, process reinvention, leveraging knowledge, and other elements of VOI?

Answers to these questions may hold the key to the future of VOI in higher education.

Using ROI/VOI in the Case Studies

The resourcing case studies in Chapter 3 utilize ROI and VOI as yardsticks to describe and examine the impacts of the activities. A number of these cases illustrate significant, current VOI benefits and/or substantial VOI in the near future.

CHAPTER **3**

Case Studies of Today's Best Practices in Resourcing

- **Overview of Case Studies**
- **The Boston Consortium**
- **Loyola Marymount University/Collegis**
- **Villanova University/Tuition Management Systems**
- **National Student Clearinghouse**
- **University of Pennsylvania/Affiliated Computer Services (ACS)**
- **The George Washington University/BearingPoint**
- **Insights About Value from the Case Studies**

Today, the state-of-the-art of resourcing is in flux, somewhere beyond traditional outsourcing and reengineering, but not yet operating to the standards of VOI portrayed in Chapter 2. Nevertheless, we have captured today's exemplary practices in a series of case studies that give the hint of the new levels of performance that will be achievable in the near future.

These case studies capture insights from the perspective of both the colleges and universities and their solutions providers/resourcing partners. Different cases illustrate different principles of resourcing, deployed in addressing a variety of objectives, issues, and/or problems. An overview of the case studies is presented on page 33, summarizing the focus of each case and the institutional participants.

These cases start with an ambitious, 13-institution consortium (The Boston Consortium) dealing with broad developmental issues and particular solutions in a range of business process areas. Two cases address business process outsourcing solutions in particular functional areas (Villanova University and University of Pennsylvania). The cases also include a full outsourcing of information technology (Loyola Marymount University) to a series of Web services solutions provided in the context of a long-term partnership (George Washington University). The examples also include what we have characterized as a digital utility (National Student Clearinghouse) providing valuable solutions to thousands of institutions, intermediaries, and enterprise users.

Terms and Concepts

CMS: Course management systems are the applications that support online management of course content, registration, grading, and other supports.

Communities of Practice: These are the formal and informal groupings of practitioners that are the repositories of knowledge on practitioner tradecraft for every business process, from learning to procurement to advising. Some communities of practice reside totally within an institution, but most include practitioners at other institutions, solution providers, and other external enterprises.

Digital Utility: When outsourcing providers remotely provide services that are dependable, inexpensive, and driven by customer needs, they become *digital utilities.*

Distributed Competencies: In a networked world, we no longer speak of core competencies but of the distributed competencies that reside throughout the enterprise and the communities of practice from which it draws insights and tradecraft. Resourcing decisions are shaped by the distributed competencies that are made available to the institution.

ERP: Enterprise resource planning systems are the tightly coupled, fully integrated applications software systems used by colleges, universities, and other enterprises.

Leaderful Organizations: Communities of practice mobilize the grassroots leadership of enterprises that is essential to success in the Knowledge Economy.

Legacy Systems: The established, long-existing applications systems of large enterprises are often called "legacy" systems.

Portal: Enterprise portals are the secure gateways through which learners, faculty, customers, staff, and other stakeholders experience and personalize the enterprise's products, services, and knowledge. Portals are key to process reinvention.

Loosely Coupled: The new generation of computing architecture, which can be more loosely coupled than traditional software applications. Web services are enabling a more loosely coupled approach to software application design, and as a result, organizational design and behavior.

Surgical Outsourcing: When a portion of a business process is deconstructed and outsourced, it constitutes cosourcing or surgical outsourcing.

Transitive Trust: In order for e-commerce to succeed, participants must have a level of trust in the authenticity and predictability of the participants, processes, and services. This is called transitive trust.

Tightly Coupled: Business systems, processes, and practices are typically tightly coupled. This is achieved through software applications that are "hard-wired" to the business process they support.

Overview of Case Studies

Leading institutions and solution providers are discovering how to enhance ROI and VOI today. Both the institutions and the solution providers are featured in these cases because they are both essential to the resourcing of business processes and solutions in higher education. These case studies illustrate different elements of the business value web in action.

Case Study	Focus of Case	Institutional Participants
The Boston Consortium	• Leadership, professional development, and empowerment • Communities of practice • Shared services – risk management, internal audit and legal, IT training, portions of staff recruiting • Assessing, memorializing, and sharing learnings from initiatives	Consortium Members – Babson College, Bentley College, Berklee College of Music, Boston College, Boston University, Brandeis University, Harvard University, MIT, Northeastern University, Olin College of Engineering, Tufts University, Wellesley College, and Wheaton College
Loyola Marymount University/ Collegis	• Full outsourcing of IT services and other academic support services • Process reinvention through accepting best practices in outsourced solutions • Strategic planning and services	Loyola Marymount University, Valencia Community College
Villanova University/ Tuition Management Systems	• Business process outsourcing (BPO) • Surgical outsourcing • Process reinvention • Transitive trust	Villanova University
National Student Clearinghouse	• Digital utility serving information providers, intermediaries and end users • Surgical outsourcing • Web services • Process reinvention • Transitive trust	Digital Utility serving thousands of institutions, employers, intermediaries, and other parties
University of Pennsylvania/ Affiliated Computer Services	• Business process outsourcing (BPO) • Capacity in a wide range of service areas	University of Pennsylvania, University of Phoenix
The George Washington University/ BearingPoint	• Long-term relationship • Expert services • Process reinvention • Technology transformation • Web services	The George Washington University

The Boston Consortium Case Study

"In times of change, the learners will inherit the earth, while the knowers will find themselves beautifully equipped to deal with the world that no longer exists."

Eric Hoffer

Mission of The Boston Consortium
The Boston Consortium for Higher Education seeks to create a collaborative environment that inspires member institutions in the development and practical implementation of innovative cost management and quality improvement ideas.

Case Study Abstract

The Boston Consortium for Higher Education, Inc., involves 13 Boston-area private institutions in a multi-faceted collaboration dedicated to enhancing services and performance and reducing the cost of education. The consortium was formed by the chief financial officers at the member institutions, who serve as its board of directors. The consortium has attracted significant grant funding and institutional support to fund its operations and support particular initiatives. It deploys proven principles of organizational development to build the competencies and motivation of individuals and teams to engage in collaborative endeavors.

These collaborations use feasibility studies to select pilot ventures for implementation. Many of these have yielded a combination of cost savings, greater revenues, and enhanced levels of service. IT training, PC procurement, facilities management, insurance, and benefits programs are a few of the services that have been enhanced and trimmed in cost. The consortium has received substantial attention for its co-sourced/shared service solutions in risk management, which will eventually incorporate internal audit and legal functions as part of a comprehensive shared risk management service.

The consortium aspires to move its members to a higher plane of development, discovering new paradigms for transformational learning and reflective practice. These will change the competencies, perspectives, and behaviors of individuals, teams, communities of practice, and member institutions. These developmental gains will eventually lead to even greater cost savings, revenue increases, and service enhancements.

Background and History

The Boston Consortium was formed to address a shared interest among private higher education institutions in the Boston area: how to make higher education affordable for all students. The consortium serves as a vehicle for member institutions to explore ways to lower costs and maintain or improve quality through collaborative action. It is unique among consortia. Rather than merely focusing on procuring goods and services at a reduced cost, The Boston Consortium aims to provide formal and informal forums and ongoing developmental experiences for participants. It aims to change perspectives and behaviors through collaboration, ultimately reducing costs and improving operation at individual campuses.

Members of The Boston Consortium:
Babson College, Bentley College, Berklee College of Music, Boston College, Boston University, Brandeis University, Harvard University, Massachusetts Institute of Technology, Northeastern University, Olin College of Engineering, Tufts University, Wellesley College, and Wheaton College.

Decision to Form a Consortium to Accelerate Collaboration.
In 1996, its first year of operation, the consortium received one-year funding from the Mellon Foundation. This was followed in 1998 by multi-year funding from the Davis Foundation, which was renewed in 2000 for an additional three years. Other grant funding has been received for specific initiatives over the past several years The consortium has evolved in an *expeditionary* manner, progressively developing a pattern of using working groups, initiatives, and special training events to craft vision, strategy, and specific initiatives around which to collaborate.

Launching Inaugural Programs.
In 1996, The Boston Consortium started along this path by forming a number of working groups focused on purchasing, telecommunications, environmental health and safety, and human resources. In its first year the consortium held its inaugural management development workshop at Babson College. In 1997, the consortium completed its first round of collaborative projects and completed a job fair, group travel arrangements, hosting of outside speakers, and energy assessments of member institutions. The purchasing group identified obstacles to group purchasing and continued to explore solutions. In its second year of operation, the consortium made its decision to incorporate as an "extraordinary" not-for-profit consortium, utilizing entrepreneurial and behavioral tools to change the competencies and cultures of its member institutions.

Hiring a Managing Director.
In 1998, The Boston Consortium hired its first managing director and staged a strategic retreat to explore its future role. New groups were formed to address facilities, information technology (IT) training, energy, and health services. In later years, other groups would be added. These developments were followed in 1999 by facilities managers establishing a group benchmarking project and the emergence of a new group focusing on benefits issues. Environmental health and safety (EH&S) audits were offered, a controllers group was formed, and the EH&S group launched two Web sites: hazardous waste and chemical hygiene. Working together, Harvard University and the consortium began a PC procurement project, and the second strategic retreat took place on "Rehearsing the Future." The Management Development Series workshops launched. In addition, IT trainees developed a preferred vendor list for classroom-based training and began investigating e-learning support.

In the future, access to collaborative tools and Web-based training will be addressed by this group.

Studying Co-Sourcing/Shared Services.
In 2000, the Olin College of Engineering, the nation's newest college, joined the consortium. Moreover, The Boston Consortium institutions evaluated the feasibility of an important initiative: carving out pharmacy benefit costs. Also in 2000, six institutions evaluated cosourcing/shared services as a means to enhance service, reduce costs, maximize resources, and best address the financial and strategic objectives of each individual participant. In 2001, the six institutions participating in the Cosourcing/Shared Services Feasibility Study agreed to move forward on two fronts: 1) implementing risk management services, and 2) pursuing the goal of creating a shared services entity. By 2002/2003, Brandeis University, Berklee College of Music, Olin College of Engineering, Wheaton College, and Wellesley College had hired a shared director of risk management. In another cosourcing/shared services initiative, the internal audit planning group developed an RFP for shared services for internal audit. An important conference on security and disaster recovery, "Data, Dialogue, and Decision Making," was convened by The Boston Consortium, the Association of Independent Colleges and Universities in Massachusetts (AICUM and the state's three other consortia – Colleges of the Fenway, Colleges of Worcester Consortium, and Five Colleges).

"Location is important – being physically close together really helps. Most of all, you need a cadre of leaders to get started. CFOs are key. They have the power to make decisions in most institutions. They see the whole institution. Start with the CFOs."

Will Reed, Past VP and CFO, Wellesley College, and Chairman Emeritus, The Boston Consortium

Elements of The Boston Consortium

During the course of its expeditionary development, The Boston Consortium has refined its core set of values. These shape the practical work of the consortium, which occurs through groups, initiatives, events, and training programs.

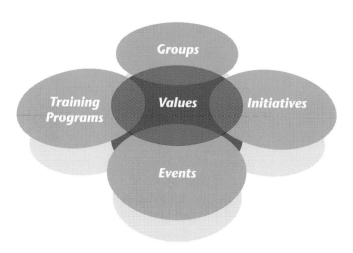

> "We need organizations that empower anyone with the capability and the willingness to assume leadership in the moment, alas, we are in it together. The essence of leadership is collaboration and mutuality."
>
> Joseph A Raelin, Asa S. Knowles Chair of Practice-Oriented Education, Northeastern University, and Counselor to The Boston Consortium

Values

The Boston Consortium has progressively refined its basic values of trust, freedom of choice, and belief in the power of collaboration and individual/organizational development.

Today's conception of these values is:

- Create trustful relationships that are the foundation of collaborative work.

- Help the colleges and universities reduce or avoid costs associated with exploration of new ideas.

- Capture the lessons learned during the dynamic process of discussion, innovation, and cooperation that takes place among consortium members.

- Respect the individuality of member institutions and their staffs.

- Build on diverse organizational strengths.

- Provide a safe place for "practice fields," experimentation, and calculated risk taking.

- Use managers' time effectively, avoiding redundant efforts and maximizing collective intellect.

- Develop pragmatic solutions that fit each institution's needs and circumstances.

- Leverage "top-down" and "bottom up" action planning.

- Create a shared language for collaboration.

- Utilize effective dialogue to advance vision of creating an extraordinary consortium.

These values will continue to evolve as the consortium discovers how to raise the capacity and change the administrative culture of its members.

Working Groups

Consortium working groups provide opportunities for professionals to meet with each other to share common interests and best practices. Over time, these working groups are expected to evolve into bona fide communities of reflective practice. More than 400 managers participate in these voluntary group activities annually. These meetings are the spawning grounds for collaborative projects, long-term partnerships, and connections with the local higher education community. Over time, these groups have grown in number and composition.

The table on the facing page profiles 16 working groups.

Working Groups

Benefits

Benefits managers meet and share collaborative ideas. Collaborative projects have included: shared training with TIAA/CREF, Dental Association Study, and the Pharmacy Carve Out Feasibility Study. A subgroup of Bentley College, Brandeis University, Wellesley College, and Wheaton College is developing long-term care programs at each of the institutions.

Environmental Health and Safety

In 1999, the EH&S Group launched a shared Web site for training the institutions' 43,000 employees on hazardous waste removal and chemical hygiene. Other activities include RCRA Web-based training and joint discussion sessions with risk managers on personal liability issues related to environmental incidents.

Board of Directors/Fiscal Officers

The chief financial officers of the member institutions compose the board of directors of The Boston Consortium.

Chief Human Resource Officers

Meeting regularly to exchange information, best practices and new developments, the chief human resource officers lead collaborative initiatives such as the Management Development series, the Dental Association study, and the Pharmacy Carve Out Feasibility Study.

Facilities Management

The Facilities Management Group has engaged in a benchmarking initiative aimed at building greater sophistication in facilities budgeting and forecasting tools. Custodial and energy costs have received attention as well. A subgroup has worked with SightLines, a facilities asset advisory firm, to share benchmarking and use a "return on physical asset"

(ROPA) model to evaluate the relationship between facility construction, plant maintenance, and service delivery.

Project Facilitators Network (PFN)

During 2000, the consortium launched the PFN, to create a cadre of trained facilitators reflecting the values of The Boston Consortium. These facilitators have been used at the consortium retreats and events, intercollegiate facilitation, and intra-school events. They have yielded both a solid ROI and a uniform, high standard of effective meetings.

Risk Management

This group engaged in conversations, which launched strategic evaluation of risk on the campuses. The Cosourcing/Shared Services initiative on Risk Management has been undertaken by a subset of this group and has moved into implementation with the hiring of a risk management director.

Controllers

The Controllers Group, formed in 1999, initially focused on understanding operations at each college or university, so that members could improve their own processes, network, and explore collaborative initiatives. They have explored using Web-based technology for financial transactions, credit card applications, purchasing card programs, and other ventures. Their current focus is on identifying best practices and common practices and discussing oncoming changes and how to prepare for them.

Health Services

The Health Services Group began meeting in 2000 to share common problems and consider development of an interactive Web site providing health services information and resources to consortium students.

Telecom

This group's key functions are to share information and best practices for possible use by other institutions and to share information on broad trends and changes in the industry to enable members to plan appropriately.

Employment

In 2001, employment managers began meeting to share information and discuss common areas of interest: job fairs, advertising, referral programs, temporary agencies, background check procedures, new hire orientation, professional search firms, and applicant tracking and database management. The Employment Managers Group is in Phase I of a Shared Recruiting Project. Six colleges and universities have committed financial support to initiate the project. This phase will provide an electronic presence on a number of targeted Web sites, including diversity and professional organizational sites.

IT Training

This group has been very active. In 2000, the IT Training Group selected Element K as its vendor for Web-based training and 10 out of 12 consortium members are taking advantage of these services, which include training in more than 300 software applications. Substantial financial savings have been realized, and seat-sharing among institutions has enhanced class balance. Tufts University and Wheaton College have led the migration to KnowledgeHub, Element K's next generation solution. An IT subgroup is evaluating Web-based collaborative solutions.

Organizational Development and Training

This group has gone through several changes in name and direction. In 2000, six colleges and universities formed a Training Collaborative and Supervisor's Certification

Program, a professional development program recognizing the value of developing leaders at all levels. The group continues to develop leadership enhancement opportunities and to share best practices at member institutions.

Purchasing

The consortium's members have shared many contracts in common, using the Massachusetts Higher Education Consortium (MHEC) and other vehicles. Subgroups of the Purchasing Group have pursued a variety of p-card and e-procurement initiatives. A pilot project with Commonfind was aborted when the vendor withdrew from the business. In 2002, the consortium board committed Davis grant monies to support a one-year pilot project, and to attract $25,000 from each participating college or university. The pilot will build on the ECAT platform at MIT, which will be adapted to individual institutions by the firm OrgSupply. Harvard University is the first participant and will share its experience with other institutions.

Sponsored Research

The Sponsored Research Group sponsored a three-day conference in June 2002 on the fundamentals of sponsored research. The program workshops were provided by the National Council of University Research Administrators (NCURA).

Public Safety Officers

The staging of the workshop, "ROI Data, Dialogue, Decision Making: Disaster Planning for Higher Education." ROI has been the signal accomplishment of this group.

Seven Steps to Collaboration

1 — Selecting Initiative
2 — Gathering Information
3 — Refining the Focus
4 — Identifying a Champion
5 — Procuring Needed Resources
6 — Putting the Parts Together
7 — Reflecting and Learning

Initiatives

Consortium initiatives are spawned by the various groups (see facing page). The fundamental philosophy of The Boston Consortium is that initiatives move the consortium from simple collaboration (Level I) to "systems thinking" through collaborative projects (Level II). Such thinking can stimulate transformational learning. Initiatives are a key part of a seven-step collaborative process used by the consortium, utilizing dialogue to build trust, which forms and strengthens relationships, enabling the team to assess and then take advantage of opportunities.

"The CFOs form the working groups but they don't specifically charge them with what to do. The working groups figure out not just the solutions, but what the problem is, what we need to know to solve it, and how to arrive at the solution through an initiative."

Diane Devlin, Manager of Strategic Procurement, Harvard University, Member of the Purchasing Group.

Events and Training Programs

Consortium events and training programs have provided formal programs to catalyze fresh thinking and a better understanding of emerging concepts. Examples have included:

- *Critical Incident Management Workshop* explored crisis management issues and techniques.

- *Creating Sustainability in Business and the Environment* reviewed planning for physical facilities construction, going beyond recycling and energy management to include utilization of environmentally friendly building materials and gauging the true cost of short-life cycle buildings.

- *Personal Liability Re: Environmental Transgression* reviewed the regulatory framework and case studies for personal environmental liability.

- *Facility Outsourcing Forum* enabled facilities professionals to explore the issues relating to outsourcing and contract management.

- *E-Commerce Workshop* gathered representatives from 11 institutions to discuss potentials for e-commerce, particularly e-procurement.

- *Health Care Cost Management Forum* engaged Charles Baker, CEO of Harvard Pilgrim Health Care (HPHC), to explore a variety of innovative approaches to health care cost control and service enhancement.

- *Disaster Planning for Higher Education* conference was held by The Boston Consortium and three other multi-institution consortia in Massachusetts.

- *Retreats* have provided an annual opportunity to convene around key issues such as "Rehearsing the Future" and "Building Collective Wisdom."

In addition to special events, The Boston Consortium stages professional development programs to augment the formal and informal learning that goes on in working groups and during special initiatives. Examples have included:

- *The Boston Consortium Management Development Series* offers workshops that are open to all consortium institution employees. In addition, MIT has offered all consortium institution employees access to their workshops, which are held at MIT's Professional Learning Center.

- *TIAA/CREF Institute* offered a series of workshops on pension plans, health and welfare plans, and fringe benefits.

Specific Initiatives

Pharmacy Carve Out

In 2000, 10 of the consortium's 12 member institutions evaluated the feasibility of carving out pharmaceutical coverage from their medical plans, determining if collaboratively purchasing prescription drug coverage would yield cost savings and/or enhance service effectiveness. The group concluded that neither of these outcomes would be realized. However, the process of collectively and systematically evaluating this idea led to insights and other avenues for the institutions to address this situation. The lessons learned from this initiative were published in "Learning History," the first of an ongoing series of white papers on important lessons learned that have been developed for and shared with the consortium community. Changing conditions have enhanced the importance of this issue. Recently, Boston University created its own pharmacy carve-out program, saving $800,000 annually.

Academic Village

In early 2001, participants from Boston College, Boston University, Bentley College, Northeastern University, and Tufts University began a feasibility study process to evaluate shared, off-balance sheet, tax-exempt graduate housing. This initiative has gone through three distinct iterations. In each, the working group conducted the feasibility study and created a workable alternative (successively called Academic Village, Collegiate Village, and Habitat for Learning). For various reasons (changing conditions, post 9/11, and other factors), no member institutions have chosen to take

advantage of these initiatives – yet. This remains a concept-in-waiting for the right confluence of circumstances.

Owner Controlled Insurance Program (OCIP)

In 2000, a number of consortium institutions collaborated to create a group Owner-Controlled Insurance Program (OCIP), which allows them to save substantial funds on construction project insurance costs and which includes pollution liability for remediation projects.

Computer Purchasing

Several consortium colleges and universities have taken advantage of reduced prices on major brands of desktop computers, printers, lease rates, and services through buying arrangements via consortium member Harvard University. This has yielded substantial savings.

SightLines

The consortium underwrote the cost of a facilities study to explore the relationship between asset investment, asset consumption, operating process, and service delivery (a concept called "return on physical assets" – ROPA). This shared tool makes it easier to identify cost savings.

Facilities Benchmarking

Working with Feeney Associates, facilities managers have worked to "get behind the numbers" to understand how to optimize their operations and cost structure.

IT Training

In 1998, the IT Training Group conducted a feasibility study of collaboratively addressing the IT training needs of consortium members. At that time, the 11 consortium institutions participating in the study were spending only $400,000, in total, on IT training, although the IT departments faced the challenge of serving a total customer base of 64,000 students, faculty, staff, alumni, parents, families of employees, business and technical customers, and other end users.

In 1999, the IT Training Group selected two preferred and three recommended IT training companies. An "IT Higher Education Learning Partnership" (IT HELP) was formed to raise consciousness about IT training needs and leverage the use of the preferred vendors. During the year between July 1, 1999, and June 30, 2000, the 11 participating colleges and universities invested nearly $250,000 in IT HELP and realized an estimated $180,000 in savings through collective buying power.

The IT Training Group has also arranged for Web-based learning services through Element K. In the summer of 2003, Tufts and Wellesley will lead the way by migrating to Element K's new product, KnowledgeHub. Another subgroup has been working on Web-based collaborative solutions that will supplement existing Web-based learning resources in the institutions.

Co-Sourcing/Shared Services

In 2000, Babson College, Bentley College, Brandeis University, Olin

College, Wellesley College, and Wheaton College evaluated the feasibility of sharing certain "backroom functions" such as risk management, internal audit, legal services, and employment services. The institutions saw potential opportunities to enhance service, reduce cost, and efficiently use resources. The first shared service selected for implementation was risk management. A $225,000 grant from the Mellon Foundation was acquired to support this expedition, and funds from the Davis Educational Foundation and the institutions will be used to support it. In 2002, consortium members Brandeis University, Berklee College of Music, the F.W. Olin College of Engineering, Wheaton College, and Wellesley College hired a shared director of risk management, who reports in a matrix fashion to the Risk Advisory Group of these institutions.

The overall plan is for the consortium to use shared services for internal audit and legal functions. These efforts are open to all institutions, but the driving force is coming from small to medium-sized colleges and universities. If the Risk Management pilot fulfills its promise, it will be weaned of grant funds and potentially formulated as a separate business entity owned and operated by the five participating institutions.

E-Procurement Pilot

The unsuccessful partnership with Commonfind has been followed by a pilot program to adapt MIT's successful e-procurement platform to other consortium institutions.

"Wisdom can stultify innovation. The more experience you have, the more you understand why something cannot be done, or won't work."

John Seely Brown

- *IP Convergent Networks Training* was offered by the Telecom Group on the opportunities for voice, data, and video running on a single IP network.

- *The Training Collaborative's Professional Development and Supervisor's Certificate Program* was offered by human resources professionals from Babson College, Boston College, Brandeis University, Wellesley College, and Wheaton College to develop competencies and insights based on the latest thinking about leadership and performance management.

- *Tuition Policy Charette* engaged fiscal officers in a statistical analysis of the impact of tuition policy under different scenarios.

- *Sponsored Research Workshop* was staged to expose research administrators to sessions prepared by the National Council of Research Administrators (NCURA).

- *Leadership Development Series ("Breakfast with Joe")* enabled The Boston Consortium staff to meet with Professor Joseph Raelin and discuss important issues of personal and working group leadership.

The Boston Consortium's mix of working groups, initiatives, events, and professional development programs is more comprehensive and complex than the offerings of most other consortium arrangements.

Key Distinguishing Features of The Boston Consortium

"There are roughly 150 consortia in higher education. Most report to the President and focus on particular cost saving initiatives. The Boston Consortium is different, reporting to the CFOs and focusing on organizational development to yield pervasive quality improvement and cost savings."

Peter McKenzie, Chairman, The Boston Consortium, and Financial Vice President & Treasurer, Boston College

The founding partners of The Boston Consortium understood that institutions need three ingredients to reduce costs, grow revenues, and enhance the services experienced by stakeholders:

- *Better strategies for creating collaboration, discovering innovative approaches, and building grassroots support*

- *Innovative solutions that utilize collaboration, technology, and new techniques to create economies of scale and intellect, pushing administrative costs down and driving quality up*

- *Aggressive development of individual, team, and institutional competencies and motivation, resulting in changes in institutional cultures*

From the start, the consortium's leaders focused on the importance of development, systems thinking, and engaging the individual's intrinsic motivation to excel. This distinctive commitment has differentiated the consortium from other higher education consortia.

The leadership of the consortia has observed a significant increase over the past several years in the serious commitment of participants to cost savings and service enhancement. The tough financial times confronting American higher education make the consortium's work even more important to the member institutions and to other institutions that can learn from the consortium's approaches.

With experience, the consortium has understood how far it has yet to go to achieve its goals of transforming the administrative service cultures of its

Figure 2 – Levels of Collaboration Within The Boston Consortium

Level	Activities	Evolution/ Process and Structure	Competency Development and Behavioral Change
Level I: Working groups, events, and initiatives Requirements to advance to level II: Developing skills and interest in greater levels of collaborative solutions	Working groups form around interest areas and attract participants. Events and training programs used to engage participants. • Information exchange • Benchmarking • Data collection • Cost reduction through leveraged scale • Minimize redundant systems, combining resources and knowledge Feasibility studies frame and shape initiatives that are offered to institutions for participation.	Evolution of working groups and initiatives • Entry-level exposures serve to introduce group process, collaboration, and mutual learning • Introduction to collaborative methodology • Operate within existing organizational paradigms Process/structure • Broad-based participation • Incremental change, shaped by transformative vision • The Boston Consortium serves as incubator • Change championed by individuals • Expeditionary initiatives	Competency development • Individual skills developed though events, workshops, and initiatives • Shared vision, perspectives, facilitation experiences • Development of working groups Behavioral change • Initiatives continue to operate within existing paradigm • Individuals begin to understand transformation and selectively decide to act differently
Level II: Collaborative projects and communities of practice Requirements to advance to level III: Commitment and competencies	Collaborative projects provide new solution opportunities • Shared systems/services in environmental health and safety, site training, risk management, IT training, and management education • Intra-institution reinforcement of collaborative values Working groups evolve into communities of practice • Autonomic learning • Perpetual development • Define problems, what must be learned, initiatives to be pursued, nature of solutions	Evolution of working groups and initiatives • Introspective learning • Facilitative methodology • Develop a transitional paradigm Process/structure • Self-selecting participation • Evolutionary change endorsed by management • Real-world application: The Boston Consortium as sponsor	Competency development • Individual skills developed through collaborative projects • Working groups evolve into communities of practice Behavioral change • More individuals operate in transitional or new patterns of behavior • Communities of practice selectively showcase new behavior – tell stories, share sagas, assess successes, failures, and next steps
Level III: Large-scale change/ efforts in improving organizational effectiveness Outcome: Diffusion of innovation and innovative thinking	Large-scale change efforts in improving organizational effectiveness • Advanced skills and management development • Demonstration projects • Entrepreneurial initiatives at institutions • Undertake more ambitious initiatives, broader institutional participation Communities of practice affect organizational effectiveness across interest areas • Spread DNA to home institutions • Change organizational dynamics	Evolution of working groups and initiatives • Transformational learning • Action learning methodology • Develop a new paradigm for collaborative initiatives • Reflective practice • More ambitious projects • Attract more participants and build their commitment Process/structure • Participation by nomination • Quantum change negotiated with management • New world application: The Boston Consortium as launching pad • Network leaders of change	Competency development • Individuals, cross-institutional working groups, and institutional teams demonstrate new competencies • Empowerment Behavioral change • Individuals, communities of practice, and institutions begin to learn and develop new solutions in transformational ways • Most staff participate in The Boston Consortium working groups

"We always wanted to save money. But we couldn't achieve our goals without developing the perspectives and capacities of staff. Sometimes the shortest distance between two points is the long way around."

Phil DiChiara, Managing Director, The Boston Consortium

members at the enterprise, team, and individual levels. Figure 2 illustrates the emerging vision of the levels of collaboration foreseen by the consortium. To date, most of the consortium's activities have been at Level I and early stage Level II. The large-scale, enterprise-wide efforts to improve effectiveness that characterize Level III are still in the future.

Demonstrable Outcomes – ROI and VOI

The consortium was founded with a crystal clear commitment to enhancing quality and reducing cost/price. It did not initially focus on performance measurement, however. Rather, it developed individual and working group perspectives/competencies which progressively spawned initiatives. Individual institutions had the option to buy into participation in the resulting solutions, and selected institutions chose to do so.

While not emphasizing performance measurement, The Boston Consortium has already demonstrated its capacity to deliver an improved ROI on its initiatives, as described in Figure 3. Through the feasibility study process, ROI is one of the clear benchmarks that is needed for an initiative to move into implementation. Even greater ROI should be attainable through future initiatives that may turn their attention to reinventing existing processes.

VOI. The Boston Consortium has also demonstrated significant VOI, as illustrated in Figure 4. The consortium's basic commitments embody the key elements of VOI: 1) creating a new kind of cross-institutional leadership, 2) nurturing collaboration and the development of communities of practice, and 3) building competencies at the individual, team, community of practice, and enterprise levels.

Figure 3 – ROI from The Boston Consortium

Elements of ROI	Already Demonstrated	Potential/Targeted
Reduced costs	• *Initiatives have demonstrated cost savings: shared service projects – risk management, IT training, shared recruiting.* • *Reduce costs of ongoing procurements of hardware/software, other IT items.*	• *Future initiatives will continue to yield savings, including shared internal audit, recruiting, and legal services; e-procurement; and others yet to emerge.*
Enhanced services, increases in revenues	• *Service enhancement has been achieved in key initiatives: IT training and risk management.* • *The consortium has succeeded in attracting significant foundation funding, in addition to support from member institutions. This has created a seed money pool of sort for ventures (initiative) and general support of the consortium.*	• *Enhanced service and performance will continue to be a target for future initiatives.* • *As the competencies and perspectives of members develop, a broader range of initiatives will be undertaken, including those in academic areas having significant opportunities for revenue enhancement.* • *The consortium will continue to attract foundation funding for key initiatives that have high demonstration value for other institutions.*

Figure 4 – VOI at The Boston Consortium

Elements and Nature of VOI	Already Demonstrated	Potential/Targeted
1. Enable new levels and kinds of leadership	• CFOs form the consortium • Leadership exercised by individuals in working groups and initiatives	• Individual and group leadership will grow – concurrent, collective, collaborative, and compassionate • At participating institutions, new leadership will affect other units
2. Support reinvention and innovation	• Selected initiatives have changed particular processes – IT training, shared services for risk management	• Process innovation and reinvention will be more widely practiced • At the institutional level, it could spread to all academic, academic support, and administrative processes
3. Formalize knowledge management and make better use of knowledge	• Professional development through the consortium makes knowledge resources and best practices available to employees	• Knowledge management, Web-based resources will continue to develop • Knowledge management advances will affect other institutional knowledge resources
4. Enable collaboration and use of communities of practice	• Consortium "dramatically and fundamentally" changes and enhances the use of collaboration among participating individuals in member institutions (largely administrative professionals) • Collaboration is the vehicle for identifying and taking advantage of opportunities for VOI enhancement	• Working groups will evolve into genuine communities of practice, enhancing the level of collaboration and reflective practice • Collaboration at the member colleges and universities will increase as the "collaborative DNA" is spread to other areas
5. Increase individual, organizational competencies	• Consortium builds competencies at individual, team, and institutional levels • Some individuals demonstrate transformational behavior and competencies	• Individual, team, and enterprise competencies will grow. Truly transformative learning and behavior will be more widespread
Nature of VOI: Organizational Impact, Scope, and Dynamics	• Scope – mostly tactical/incremental, some strategic • Organizational impact – individual performance, some enterprise performance • Dynamics – productivity, collaboration, some innovation	• Scope – strategic/transformational • Organizational impact – enhance strategic direction – achieve competitive advantage • Dynamics – productivity, collaboration, and innovation

Focus on Key Insights

The Boston Consortium is different from both other consortia and single-issue collaborative ventures between groups of institutions. It is different from other CFO-sponsored cost saving or BPO initiatives. The work of the consortium is demonstrating that the capabilities of staff and their relationships are the key to unlocking the value resident in institutional processes and programs.

The real story at The Boston Consortium is that the CFOs have committed themselves to the personal and professional development, commitment, and passion of their staffs as the key ingredients in discovering effective new solutions and saving money.

The following insights highlight the distinctiveness of the consortium and how that is reflected in its initiatives and byproducts.

Leadership Development

The consortium develops a different kind of leadership that is spread throughout the organization. It emphasizes concurrent action on many fronts, rather than serial progress on successive initiatives. Collective rather than individual leadership is encouraged through working groups. The consortium is collaborative instead of controlling, and compassionate rather than dispassionate. It uses Joseph Raelin's notion of "leaderful" organizations to capture the essence of what is required to succeed in today's higher education environment. This concept of leadership holds that communities of practice mobilize the grassroots leadership of enterprises that is essential to success in the Knowledge Economy.

A Generative, Organic Experience

Staff at consortium institutions have opportunities to function on a larger playing field. The working groups and initiatives often engage staff in addressing a broader set of issues, at a higher level, than would be possible given their individual job description. By working on problems from a multi-institutional perspective, staff develop skills in deconstructing processes and separating the essence of a function from its form, the real value from the effects of

Continua of Leadership in Organizations

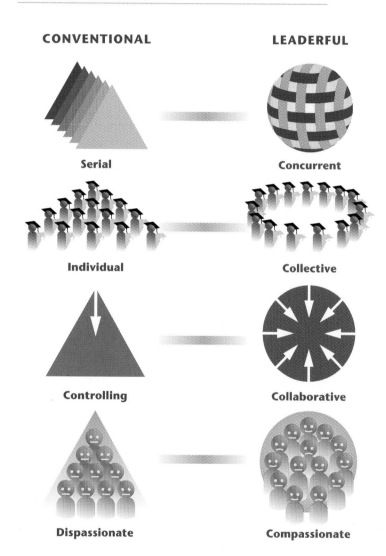

CONVENTIONAL   LEADERFUL

Serial   Concurrent

Individual   Collective

Controlling   Collaborative

Dispassionate   Compassionate

Source: Joseph L Raelin. "Creating Leaderful Organizations: How to Bring Out Leadership in Everyone." p.4

Operating Principles of The Boston Consortium

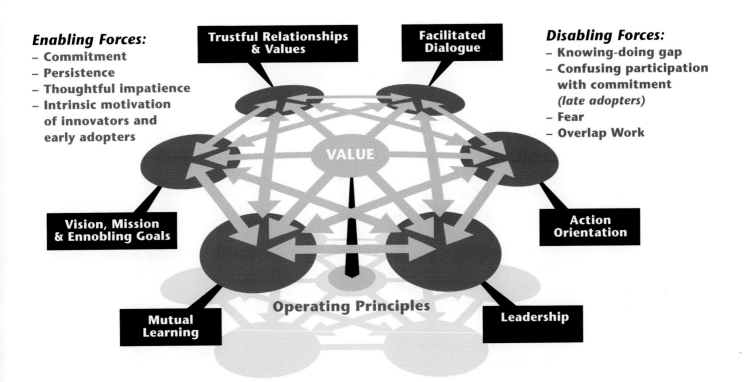

Enabling Forces:
- Commitment
- Persistence
- Thoughtful impatience
- Intrinsic motivation of innovators and early adopters

Disabling Forces:
- Knowing-doing gap
- Confusing participation with commitment (late adopters)
- Fear
- Overlap Work

tradition and culture. Functioning in the open, team-oriented environment of the consortium expands promotional opportunities for individual staff, and enables joint recruiting to attract fresh talent.

"The work of The Boston Consortium often requires a radical change in one's mindset. For the professional administrative staff, it means figuring out how to deliver the best and most cost effective service by venturing beyond the confines of one's institution. When top management embraces the goals of The Boston Consortium, performance reviews have an added dimension – how well does the individual cooperate with their professional colleagues, how open are they to new ideas, how clever are they in using all of The Boston Consortium's resources at their disposal."

Will Reed, Past VP and CFO, Wellesley College, and Chairman Emeritus, The Boston Consortium

Over time the consortium has refined its operating principles to capture the essence of its principles. It has also identified the enabling forces that support its mission and the disabling forces that stand in its way.

Different Twist on Familiar Initiatives – Risk Management

Many institutions and consortia have undertaken the sharing of a risk management professional among multiple institutions. Characteristically, The Boston Consortium has taken a different, more ambitious tack. First, it has defined the issue more expansively. Risk management is conceived as a gateway to a broad range of services, including internal audit and legal services. While the initial creation of a shared risk management service involved the hiring of a risk manager, over time his portfolio will include internal audit and legal services and will integrate risk management into literally every aspect of institutional life, every business process.

"Participating in the Risk Management Initiative gave me and other staff the capacity to demonstrate and build our capabilities in a far broader range of areas than we would have experienced otherwise. This really builds commitment, confidence, and morale."

Linda Murphy Church, Associate VP, Wellesley College, member Risk Management Advisory Committee

"We have elevated the professional staffs' thinking about their position in their institution. They are not locked within the confines of a single system. They think of themselves as professionals. As a group they are less provincial. They have more options, more ideas, and a heightened sense of new ways to be creative. They support each other, they build friendships, and they realize that collectively they can do more and have more fun. This has elevated the whole system."

Will Reed, Past VP and CFO, Wellesley College and Chairman Emeritus, The Boston Consortium

The risk manager leads a Consortium Risk Management Team whose individual members report to the CFOs of their respective campuses. These individuals have been exposed to a broad and interconnected set of issues, creating a significant developmental opportunity for them.

The second major difference is that in selecting a broker and insurance underwriters, the Risk Management Team emphasized the firms' capacities to understand the consortium culture, use benchmarking and best practices, respond entrepreneurially and creatively, and develop lines of business meeting the consortium's unique needs. The incumbent firms were insufficiently insightful and failed to make the cut. As one of its first actions under these new relationships, the consortium has increased the transactional efficiency by moving to a common anniversary date for its lines of insurance.

Challenges, Risks, and Threats

Despite its initial accomplishments and promise of even greater successes, the consortium faces several challenges, threats and risks:

- The consortium works hard to assure that its working groups and initiatives are not an extra layer of work on top of normal staff assignments. If the work becomes overwhelming, participation of staff could waver.

- To this point, innovators and early adopters have been the primary participants, Attracting late adopters and achieving their genuine commitment, rather than mere participation, is a challenge.

- Working groups need to consolidate and enhance their status as communities of practice, taking on more substantial projects and memorializing accomplishments. This will be challenging.

- Many potential business partners have been insufficiently creative to respond effectively to the opportunities provided by the consortium. Corporate responses to the Pharmacy Carve Out were disappointing. Some of these issues may be revisited in the future.

- The consortium is receiving many offers to include other groups of institutions in its activities and/or to apprentice other groups in how to do it. If managed poorly, responding to these requests could dilute efforts.

These challenges are part of a bigger picture, which includes substantial future opportunities.

What the Future Holds

The Boston Consortium is at an interesting juncture in its evolution. The confluence of several forces will likely accelerate the consortium's development and visibility.

The consortium has been quietly using its first years of development to evolve its values, working groups, initiatives, and events/professional development experiences in an expeditionary manner. Its developmental approach and several of its signature initiatives are beginning to attract substantial attention.

Moreover, over the past several years member institutions have become even more serious about cutting costs and enhancing services, given the financial crisis gripping American higher education.

"When we started The Boston Consortium, some schools were on hard times. But then came the glorious times of the late 1990s. But the burning times have come again and that will stimulate new interest in cooperative enterprises and more ambitious solutions. Bad financial environments require more serious attention to business issues."

*Peter McKenzie,
Chairman, The Boston Consortium*

The greater appreciation of the power of collaboration and the development of new community-of-practice competencies and knowledge sharing tools will likely accelerate the consortium's development.

Understanding and Measuring Performance and Value

In its early years, the consortium focused on developing the culture, commitment, and capacity necessary to enhance quality and reduce costs across its member institutions. Now that a cadre of developed leaders has experienced the fulfillment of participating and succeeding, the opportunity is ripe for assessment and reflection to understand where the consortium has enhanced value and where potential value resides in other processes and activities. Performance measurement is likely to be an important issue for the consortium over the next few years. Also, storytelling will be important within the consortium to engage participants in understanding value.

New Leadership and Staff Participation

The consortium has empowered a second generation of senior leadership, beyond the group of "founding fathers" who launched the effort in the mid 1990s. This is a significant passage. Further, the participating staff in the efforts of working groups and initiatives need to be expanded to reach a broader cross section of institutional staffs – not just the innovators and the early adopters, but the late adopters who need to become committed if the consortium is to achieve its potential.

New Initiatives, New Partners, New Horizons, Bright Future

The CFOs and grassroots leadership of the consortium are considering a diverse palette of new opportunities. Some are new endeavors. Others are revisitations or extensions of earlier efforts. One of the greatest opportunities confronting the consortium involves disseminating its best practices to other institutions or consortia. The consortium's foundation funding carries the responsibility to promote the spread of collaborative, leaderful efforts to enhance quality and reduce costs. By telling its story and mentoring other consortia groups, The Boston Consortium will further hone its members' understanding of how to optimize value in the business processes of colleges and universities. A new wave of initiatives will certainly follow.

The Boston Consortium is dedicated to sharing the principles of collaborative, leaderful efforts to enhance quality and reduce costs.

Loyola Marymount University/Collegis Case Study

Case Study Abstract

Loyola Marymount University (LMU) engaged Collegis to audit its IT capabilities, then to outsource the IT enterprise. LMU signed a seven-year contract with Collegis, which made Collegis and LMU strategic partners in addressing the university's deployment of technology. Starting in January 2002, Collegis assumed responsibility for consolidating IT budgets; employing and managing a consolidated IT department; leveraging experienced regional, national, and corporate management; providing as needed, "just-in-time" corporate expertise and support; facilitating the development of administrative and instructional technology action plans; ensuring a flexible and reliable infrastructure that will support expansion at LMU; implementing "best practices" and proven methodologies; and delivering reliable and responsive user support, professional development, and training.

Collegis is a technology services and solutions company serving 110 institutions of higher education. Its business offerings include strategic services, technology management solutions, learning technology solutions, and curriculum solutions. Collegis works at the presidential level to craft relationships and build solutions using administrative systems, computing infrastructure, and learning technologies. Its value proposition focuses on managing the cost and return on technology investments, using Internet technology for teaching and learning, developing new revenue sources, attracting and retaining students, faculty, and technology staff, and being responsive to today's competitive landscape.

*Loyola Marymount's Strategic Intent:
Loyola Marymount University will become the preeminent Catholic University in the Western United States. To achieve this goal, LMU's leadership realized they must dramatically enhance their information and communications technology capabilities.*

Loyola Marymount University

Loyola Marymount University (LMU) is the only Jesuit and Marymount Catholic university in Los Angeles, balancing a strong liberal arts and sciences curriculum and a commitment to strong ethical and social values. It enrolls 5,358 undergraduates, 1,446 graduate students and another 1,411 in its Law School. Its 350 faculty and 1,500 full-time and part-time employees occupy a pleasant campus near the Pacific Ocean.

Decision to Seek Expert Services Assistance. In 2001, Loyola Marymount University completed a comprehensive institutional strategic planning process resulting in a vision of LMU becoming the preeminent Catholic university in the Western United States. The university's strategic plan identified a variety of major initiatives that would be needed to achieve this vision, including the need to enhance the university's use of information technology because of the substantial and growing role technology plays in the day-to-day life of the university's faculty, staff, and external constituents.

Using the university strategic plan as a foundation, LMU contracted with Collegis to conduct a comprehensive assessment of LMU's use of information technology and to lead a college-wide IT strategic planning effort. The resulting IT strategic plan included the following seven IT strategic goals:

1. Provide technology leadership with authority in policy-making and budgeting, with a mandate to develop and implement in an integrated technology plan;

2. Secure and allocate adequate resources to meet the IT needs of LMU;

3. Provide seamless, easy, and anytime/anywhere access to integrated, secure, and reliable LMU systems;

4. Ensure that all LMU buildings and facilities have appropriate state-of-the-art IT infrastructure;

5. Establish a technology training and support program that is timely, and responsive to broad and specialized needs and keeps pace with ever-changing requirements;

6. Provide students with relevant resources and services to promote learning and community; and

7. Use the capabilities of technology to foster effective relationships between LMU and its external constituencies.

The IT strategic planning team also determined that LMU could not move forward on these goals without fixing some profound shortcomings in the institution's technology infrastructures and capabilities. A variety of perspectives shaped the conversation, including input from board members experienced in the successful use of technology.

The decision to outsource the management of information technology at LMU flowed from the results of the assessment, the planning effort, and the university's realization that external assistance was necessary if the university was to achieve its goals. The decision to outsource was made in January 2002, and the actual contract was put in place on February 1, 2002.

Collegis at a Glance

Collegis is an example of a technology-based services company that has responded to the new conditions, contexts, and technologies in higher education by expanding and extending the scope, nature and focus of its services. Collegis has built its value proposition on two primary foundations: 1) its traditional services base in outsourced IT services and 2) the market-leading academic support services of Eduprise, which was brought back into the company to create a broader range of academic and administrative offerings. As a result, Collegis offers four categories of service (LMU does not use all of these services):

• **Strategic Services** including assessments, planning, business process redesign, and market and branding strategy;

• **Technology Management Solutions** such as on-site technology management, on-site help desk operations and remote support, on-site and remote network management, application management and support, and Web design and support;

• **Learning Technology Solutions** encompass learning technology management, faculty and student support, instructional development services, infrastructure and network support, and enterprise application integration; and

Collegis Mission: Collegis is the leading provider of comprehensive business, technology, and curriculum services for higher education. Its motto is "Higher Education Through Technology."

"On many occasions, Collegis is approached by institutions whose entire focus is on what type of technology they want to buy. At Loyola Marymount University, the focus from the beginning has been on what the university is trying to strategically accomplish and how technology can support the institution's vision, mission, and goals. This strategic view of technology makes LMU a perfect partner for Collegis since we are vendor neutral and implement most hardware and software support systems."

Jan Baltzer, Collegis Senior VP for Strategic Services

- **Curriculum Solutions** include providing learner-centric instruction for continuing education students, increasing enrollments and revenues through services such as outsourced management and administration, complete curriculum materials, supplemental marketing and student recruitment, blending of e-education benefits with instructor-led delivery, and instructional mentoring.

This set of services is of a sufficiently strategic nature that campus decision making is at the presidential level. These services are centered on the evaluation, selection, deployment, and management of several key technologies and the applications/programs using them:

- **Administrative systems** including student, financial, human resources, and enterprise portals;

- **Computing infrastructure** such as data centers, networks, wireless, and computing devices; and

- **Learning technologies** such as course management systems, smart classrooms, computer labs, and curriculum content.

Collegis is "technology neutral and vendor independent," supporting the technology products of a wide range of vendors and addressing several key issues for colleges and universities:

- **Managing the cost and return on technology investment,** reducing academic costs (reduced cost/student, and seeking savings on hardware/software acquisition) and administrative costs (savings on hardware/software acquisition, reduction in end user support costs, reduced maintenance costs).

- **Using Internet technology for teaching and learning,** developing the capacity of the institution to weave e-learning into its offerings, serving both existing and new learners.

- **Developing new revenue sources** in the academic (increased enrollments, new program development/acquisition, and increased credit hours/student) and administrative (timely processing of financial transactions – revenue receipts and financial aid – and increased funding from sources such as alumni and grants) areas.

- **Attracting and retaining students, faculty, and technology staff.**

- **Being responsive to today's competitive higher education landscape.** Providing strategic advantage through improved teaching and learning, enhanced communications and relations, and enhanced prestige and reputation.

Collegis serves over 110 institutions of higher education. One of the best case study to demonstrate the full range of services offered is Loyola Marymount University.

Issues That Were Addressed.
LMU was typical of many institutions that had, historically, not made IT a strategic priority. Investment in IT had been fragmented. Academic computing reported to the academic vice president and administrative computing to the vice president for business and finance. Communication and collaboration was inadequate. There was serious investment in desktop computing but no natural champion for infrastructure and the campus network backbone. It was clear that all IT should report to a single executive, but it was not clear whether a chief information officer (CIO) was the answer. The campus had not developed keen insights on development and deployment of IT as a strategic asset.

The Collegis proposal to outsource IT addressed the key issues at LMU identified during the assessment and planning efforts. There was no shared vision of how IT should add value to the university; the IT governance and organizational structures were not working as efficiently or effectively as they should; academic applications of technology were inconsistent across the university; there were significant issues related to the university's infrastructure and use of the WWW; planning and budgeting for information technology were not effectively linked; and administrative systems were not functioning as effectively as they should. The proposal also clearly identified the consequences if the university failed to address these issues decisively, including higher total cost of ownership, less-than-desirable return on investment, lost productivity, user dissatisfaction, and potential damage to the university's reputation.

LMU essentially faced three choices:
1) Continue on the current path, failing to make IT a strategic priority; 2) Make IT a strategic priority but attempt to do it themselves; and 3) Contract with a firm to make IT a strategic priority.

Nature of Solution and Current Status.
LMU signed a seven-year contract with Collegis to address the university's deployment and support of information technology. The arrangement provides that Collegis:

• Provide leadership for consolidating IT budgets to achieve savings that can be reallocated for strategic initiatives, thus reducing overall IT spending as a percentage of the total operating budget;

• Employ and manage a consolidated IT department, combining academic and administrative IT professionals;

• Leverage experienced regional, national, and corporate management;

• Provide as needed, "just-in-time" corporate expertise and support;

• Facilitate the development of administrative and instructional technology action plans;

• Ensure a flexible and reliable infrastructure that will support expansion at LMU;

• Implement "best practices" and proven methodologies; and

• Deliver reliable and responsive user support, professional development and training.

Demonstrable Outcomes.
LMU is very much a work in progress, but it is an excellent example of the new kind of comprehensive, strategic resourcing arrangements that colleges and universities are considering in the face of the need to make IT a strategic priority, overcome fragmentation and dissipation of resources, and reinvent structures, processes and cultures relating to the use of IT and the resulting applications to teaching and learning.

"We generally find that institutions want to partner with us for one of two reasons: they want to incorporate a vision or they want to relieve the pain of IT systems that aren't working. In the case of LMU, they clearly had a vision of what they wanted to become and ramping up their technology was a key component in taking the institution to that next level of excellence."

Tom Huber, Collegis President & CEO

"This technology agreement is an important milestone for LMU and one of several major initiatives we will be undertaking over the next few years as we pursue our goal of becoming one of the nation's most distinguished Catholic universities. We recognize that technology is a critical enabler of everything we do and is essential to successfully realizing our strategic initiatives as a center of learning and thought in one of the world's greatest cities, Los Angeles."

Rev. Robert B. Lawton, S.J., President, Loyola Marymount University

The Collegis contract with LMU is focused on providing leadership and support to enable the university to achieve unique and measurable strategic objectives, including:

- **Improve teaching and learning** providing high levels of accessibility and quality service and increasing the effective use of LMU's IT investment through faculty training and development;

- **Improve communications and relationships** through alumni technology support and programs and increased use of the Web for communication with stakeholders;

- **Increase LMU's capacity to adapt to changing conditions** shifting spending from maintenance to innovation and increasing the speed of technology deployment; and

- **Improve the alignment of IT with institutional vision, mission, and goals** by linking planning and budgeting and achieving broad-based buy-in for IT objectives.

One of Collegis' advantages is its capacity to emphasize measurement and accountability. It can measure hundreds of performance indicators and compare performance to other institutional clients. Collegis focuses its measurements on financial return, strategic advantage, and operational improvement. These can be translated into return on investment (ROI) and value on investment VOI measurements.

The first table on the facing page compares the currently demonstrated and potential/targeted elements of Return on Investment (ROI) at LMU. The second table addresses the more intangible elements of Value on Investment (VOI) for LMU.

What the Future Holds

Collegis and LMU are at the formative stage in their relationship where Collegis is busy implementing their best practices and acquainting campus users with new structures, processes and ways of doing things. Collegis has demonstrated its capacity to lift the performance and effectiveness of campus IT operations.

Experiences from Other Institutions. While Loyola Marymount University is at a formative stage in its relationship with Collegis, other institutions are farther along the development track.

Valencia Community College has been utilizing Eduprise/Collegis services since the late 1990s. Currently, Collegis has a multi-year agreement to provide on-site technology management and staff to support academic and administrative computing activities and to support online initiatives. Dr. Sandy Shugart, president of Valencia Community College, summarized the benefits of the Collegis partnership concisely:

"Our relationship with Collegis has enabled us to move very quickly on all technology fronts. The well-balanced and integrated solutions and professional team saved the college money, hassle, and lost productivity. However, the real payoff is better service."

Three types of outcomes were especially useful, from the president's perspective:

- Collegis brought a balance of skills and perspectives in administrative systems, software, hardware, and network that are hard to find outside this kind of solutions partner.

- The relationship simplified human resources issues associated with technology. Educational institutions sometimes have difficulty in attracting ICT

Demonstrated and Potential/Targeted Elements of ROI

Elements of ROI	Already Demonstrated	Potential/Targeted
Reduced costs	• *Reduce costs of ongoing procurements of hardware/software*	• *Reduced cost per student for IT services and academic/administrative services supported by IT* • *Savings on hardware and software acquisition on both academic and administrative* • *Reduction in end-user support costs* • *Reduced maintenance costs*

Intangible Elements of VOI

Elements of VOI	Already Demonstrated	Potential/Targeted
Enable new levels and kinds of leadership	• *Aggressive, decisive leadership to make strategic commitment to IT and its use* • *Investment of leadership energy required to make the transition to outsourced IT*	• *Reduction in risk of IT support will enable leadership to focus less on correcting inadequacies in IT services and more on strategic use of IT* • *Use IT to achieve and sustain the university's vision and goals, establishing competitive advantage*
Support reinvention and innovation of processes, culture, and products/services	• *Deploy best practices in governance, organization, policies, strategic planning, and culture within the Collegis-managed IT organization* • *Express strategic intent to transform campus processes, culture, and products, services and experiences*	• *Over time, transform the campus culture relating to the use of IT in teaching/learning, academic support and administrative services* • *Use improved ERP to support the reinvention of administrative processes at LMU* • *Develop LMU's capacities in technology-supported learning, enhancing, enriching and extending learning experiences for students.*
Enable collaboration and use of communities of practice	• *Deploy management best practices and utilize collaboration with technical, management, and application resources throughout the university, as needed.*	• *Participate in Collegis user groups and special interest communities* • *Through Collegis staff and also directly, collaborate with other campus problem solvers addressing similar issues*
Increase individual and organizational competencies	• *Put in place a competent, highly skilled IT team for LMU and provide access to specialized Collegis resources and competencies*	• *Maintain a competent, highly skilled IT team and provide appropriate access to specialized Collegis resources and competencies.* • *Develop the skills of LMU faculty, staff, students, and other stakeholders to successfully use IT as a critical tool in teaching, learning, academic support, and administrative functions.* • *Enhance LMU's operation effectiveness in the increased availability and use of technology and improved service, productivity and efficiency.*

"This was and is a strategic partnership. Valencia did not enter this agreement in order to save money. We are not uninterested in that, but that is not the primary focus of this work. We need to deliver a much higher level of service and results both inside and outside the college. We chose Collegis for that reason."

Sandy Shugart, President, Valencia Community College

talent and administering benefits; it may be more effective to go with a partner that is continuously hiring top talent and providing attractive career paths.

• Collegis enabled Valencia Community College to achieve desirable turnover in technology staff and create an atmosphere of renewal, rather than longevity.

Valencia Community College is working hard on perfecting its model of student engagement to improve retention and enhance value. It is aggressively reinventing processes. The capabilities provided by Collegis are essential to these efforts. Valencia is a dominant competitive force in its marketplace. It is utilizing its core competencies to create new streams of revenue. These include: 1) learning services to corporations based locally, but having branch operations all over the nation and even the world; and 2) content and knowledge resources offered through several spin-off companies and sold to other community colleges and learning enterprises.

Villanova University/Tuition Management Systems Case Study

Case Study Abstract

This case study describes how Villanova University and Tuition Management Systems (TMS) used a combination of internal and external resources to propel the delivery of integrated tuition payment solutions to students and families at Villanova through a unique business model developed by TMS.

The business model presents a solution to the challenge of delivering a clear proven education payment path to students and families as they wrestle with the challenges of finding the best solution in an efficient and timely manner. By recognizing the power of delivering a consistent quality experience and service level across all channels (direct mail, Web, IVR, inbound phone, outbound phone, on-campus), TMS and Villanova were able to deliver significant value to students, families, and ultimately, the institution.

Beyond business processing outsourcing, this case study demonstrates the power of a true resourcing relationship between quality organizations with a real commitment to higher education and a demonstrated focus on client service. This resulted in a new competitive advantage for the institution.

Villanova and its students have experienced substantial benefits by resourcing the delivery of tuition payment solutions to Tuition Management Systems. It expanded customer service and the financial situation for families (better payment solutions, combination strategies, and the right lenders) and the institution (improved cash flow, reduction of merchant fees, and consolidation of plans). This "true partnership" has given Villanova the opportunity to leverage TMS resources to expand the institution's administrative capacity, a result that the university could not easily achieve on its own.

TMS, a business process resourcer of tuition payment solutions, has helped partner schools, colleges, and universities leverage a unique combination of talented people, effective and efficient processes, and technology/systems dedicated to helping students, families, and staff achieve the institutional mission.

Solving the Problem of Student Payment Planning

Many entering freshmen gradually go from euphoria to shock. From the thrill of being admitted, they proceed to the daunting task of dealing with the cost. They learn to speak a new language which includes acronyms such as FAFSA, SAR, EFC, and FFELP. They seek grant money but also must consider the reality that much of the funding that is available to students takes the form of loans. They hear of Perkins, Stafford, and something called PLUS; and read about payment plans and a wave of "alternative" loan products promising to provide the necessary funding.

The reality that faces most students is that they are not prepared to deal with the information overload that they face when attempting to answer the question, "How do I pay the bill?" The financial aid package is a good start. It contains information about programs but in many cases this information results in as many questions from students and parents as it answers. Where to now? Back to admissions? Of course not. How about financial aid? Been there, done that. So who can help?

The organizational structure of many institutions too often remains a series of functional units or "silos." Supporting disparate business processes, distinct internal systems, and different delivery channels tend to optimize the "silos" and not the process. In some cases, certain business processes may even be at odds with the needs of other functional silos serving the same customer (students and their families). Confusion, disappointment, and frustration often result. The following graphic illustrates the functional silos, a broad solution portfolio, and multiple distribution channels confronting students and families attempting to navigate the administrative services processes. As a result, students and families are often left on their own with no clear roadmap or proven path, no trusted counselor to whom they can turn. Many institutions have attempted to bridge this missing link by reorganizing, sponsoring major system integration initiatives, or seeking out a single business partner "who can do it all," a full solution BPO approach.

The challenge to the institution is to deliver payment counseling across multiple channels, through multiple campus offices, and to ensure that the preferred solutions are utilized, all while avoiding significant new investments of limited resources.

Traditional Approaches to Solving This Problem.
Getting the bill paid, helping families figure out sustainable payment solutions, and navigating through the bureaucratic maze of our institutions are not new problems. These are challenges colleges and universities have wrestled with for several years. Yet not many solutions have been identified to date. The traditional approaches have taken one of three paths:

- physical and/or organizational alignment, creating student one-stop shopping;

- systems integration of back-office and other applications; or

- engaging comprehensive outsourced software/service providers.

Each of the traditional approaches has had positive results on selected campuses. Many have been disappointed in what they have delivered, however. Physical and/or organizational alignment have often been thwarted by several obstacles: money, culture, and politics. The organizational complexity of "one-stop shopping" solutions has proven daunting. In addition, major system integration projects have proved problematic. Competing functional requirements, procedural protocols, and proprietary standards across these different system solutions often create an integration challenge that can be difficult to resolve. Too often the cost involved in such integration initiatives has proven prohibitive.

Defining "Payment Counseling"
Consider the following timeline:

With the delivery of the financial aid award package, students and parents become aware of their "Expected Family Contribution," their EFC. What often follows next is a bill with a due date. This is where the confusion and frustration can peak. It is a logical time to provide help in developing the best financing and payment solution for the student through "payment counseling." The payment solutions developed need to consider institutional cash flow, other student and family assets, payment plans, preferred loan products, and, often, combinations of all of these.

The Traditional Model

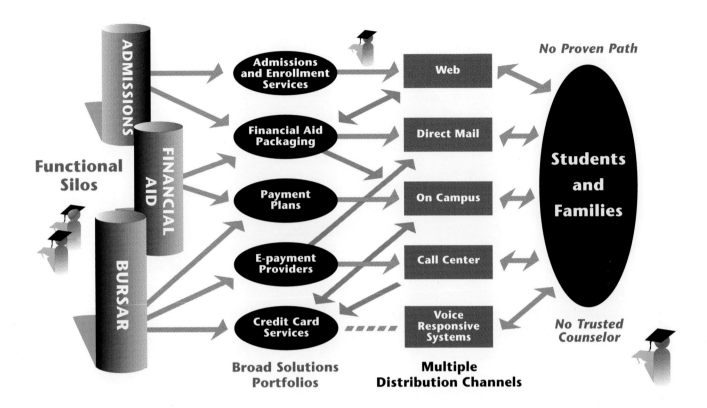

Comprehensive software/service providers offer a suite of solutions to these challenges that are broad in scope and rich in functionality. The draw is clear: the integrated delivery of solutions across multiple channels. What is often sacrificed is also clear: independence, flexibility, best in class, and leveraging legacy solutions that still fill specific needs. Committing to a broad solution set offered by a single software/service provider may commit an institution to that provider's own vision and goals. In time, as new approaches emerge and become recognized as best practices, such an institution may find that it cannot take advantage of these opportunities because of inflexibility or conflicting priorities with its software/service provider.

The "Resourcing" Approach

There are other alternatives. The process of helping families develop payment solutions that get the bill paid, does not need to be obtuse to the customer or costly to the institution. Business partners have emerged that can deliver integrated, independent payment counseling across multiple channels, leverage existing solution portfolios, and ensure that the payment solutions developed reflect the institution's preferred products and services. Integration means the delivery of a consistent solution and service across direct mail, Web, and call center channels. Independence ensures that the professional staff who counsel students and families on the best payment solutions available can fairly and accurately represent the institution's preferred lending products.

The process of helping families develop payment solutions that get the bills paid, does not need to be obtuse to the customer or costly to the institution.

A New Business Model

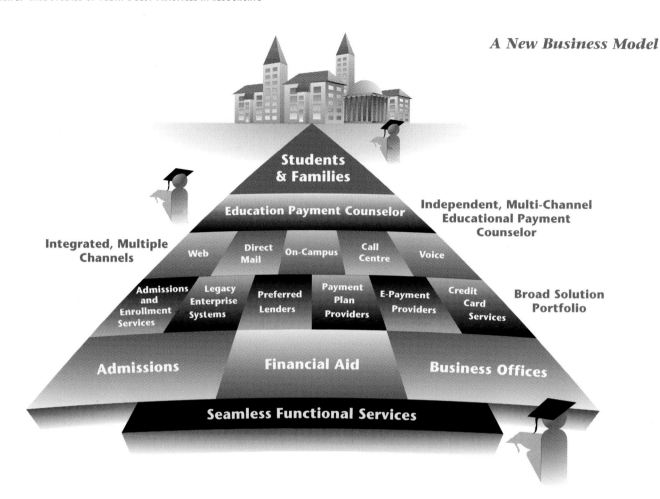

TMS Mission Statement:

Tuition Management Systems provides tuition payment solutions for more than 200,000 students and families annually at mare than 700 schools, colleges, and universities, TMS serves as educational payment counselor for students and their families.

Institutions can overcome the challenges of functional silos, leverage their existing solution portfolio, and present a consistent face to their customers across multiple channels by embracing a new business model being offered by partners such as Tuition Management Systems: independent, multi-channel education payment counseling. Through the appropriate use of enabling technologies such as Web services and an open application architecture, institutions have been able to deliver payment solutions to families that help them afford education and ensure that the bill gets paid. We will review the approach taken by Villanova University, which was seeking a partner to support its financial assistance strategy.

Villanova University

Villanova University has, over the past 10 years, taken steps to enhance services to students and families and provide a seamless administrative structure aimed at minimizing time spent by students on tasks not related to their academic pursuits (e.g., bill payment). Through increased organizational efficiencies, systems integration, and technology-based solutions, Villanova has attempted to create a "no stop shopping" approach that provides students and their families with a virtual student service center. By entering into a partnership with PNC Bank and Tuition Management Systems, Villanova University has been able to provide payment solutions grounded in an integrated counseling model to serve students more effectively.

Villanova's Goals.

Villanova sought to enhance the services provided to current and prospective students seeking the best payment solution. In addition, the university was concerned with the effectiveness, level of participation, and cost to the campus of its tuition payment solutions set, including monthly payment plans, loans, counseling, and payment methods.

Villanova's leadership wanted to provide comprehensive payment counseling to students and families that need assistance in developing the best plan to get the bill paid by finding an independent partner to objectively support its financial assistance strategy and augment the counseling services to students and families.

They believed more students and families should be taking advantage of interest-free payment plans to limit borrowing. When borrowing was necessary, they wanted a partner to direct families to the best options available for their financial needs.

Among the goals identified by the university, the following were of paramount importance:

- Provide a single point of contact to its students and families for financial aid, payment plan, and preferred lender services, simplifying navigation.

- Develop the best solutions for students and families, leveraging payment plans, then federal loan products, combinations of both, and finally, alternative loans.

- Encourage families to view a payment plan as their first step in developing a payment strategy.

- Bridge the funding gap that Villanova faced, also requiring improvements in the institution's cash flow.

- Provide students and families with anytime, anywhere access to the products and services being offered. The institution needed a partner to help it deliver the solution set across multiple channels.

Solutions to Help Villanova Prosper.

Tuition Management Systems has developed services designed to address each institution's individual needs, and these products and services were tailored to solve Villanova's particular important challenges:

- Tuition Management Systems developed a partnership with Villanova to customize a payment plan and counseling model that met its needs.

- Utilizing its counseling services and technology to find the best combination of a loan and payment plan for families, Tuition Management Systems assisted Villanova in reducing alternative loan borrowing while PLUS volume increased with its preferred lender partner. More participants in the payment plan, along with the more favorable rates on the preferred PLUS loan, helps Villanova save its families hundreds of thousands of dollars in interest charges. Services were also dramatically improved on various levels: e-payment, insurance, phone counseling, reporting, customized Web linking, and many more.

- TMS partnered with Villanova's preferred lender, PNC Bank, to address the need for a seamless integration of counseling and payment services solutions. Its team worked hand-in-hand with Villanova administrators to develop a marketing strategy based on individual needs. The initial stages included direct mail campaigns that marketed the payment plan options and were targeted to distinct student groups (e.g. undergraduates, graduate school, law school).

Villanova's Profile.

Villanova University is a comprehensive Roman Catholic institution that welcomes students of all faiths. Founded in 1842 by the friars of the Order of St. Augustine, the university offers a wide variety of degrees through four colleges: the College of Liberal Arts and Sciences, the College of Commerce and Finance, the College of Engineering, and the College of Nursing. More than 6,000 students enroll as full-time undergraduate students. A graduate enrollment (including the School of Law) of more than 3,000 and a part-time student population of approximately 700 result in a total enrollment of more than 10,000.

Demonstrable Outcomes of the Villanova/TMS Case

Elements of ROI	Already Demonstrated	Potential/Targeted
Reduced Costs for Families	• Multi-channel counseling services and technology provides families with better payment solutions, combination strategies, and the right lenders.	• Aggressively improve workflow and performance of financial and accounting systems. • Further reduce costs of information generation and deployment of special reports.
Reduced Institutional Costs	• Villanova's cash flow increased by about half a million dollars in both June and July, when they need it most. • With increased participation in payment plans, merchant fees have been reduced. • This integrated resourcing approach enabled Villanova to eliminate a separate deferred plan that formerly served its Graduate Studies population. • Jointly developed, with PNC Bank and Villanova, an early outreach Financing Plan package providing in formation and examples for paying the education bill. This is distributed as early as March to aid applicants and reduced Villanova 's summer workload and cash flow problems related to last-minute payers. • The utilization of self-service channels has increased.	• Proactive outbound counseling will be deployed from TMS' counseling center. • E-payment services will be integrated at no cost to Villanova. • Budget reconciliation will be eliminated.
Enhanced Services, Increases in Revenues	• Payment plan participation is at an all time high and borrowing has been redirected to preferred lending products. • Complete life insurance is helping students finish their education and the university to avoid write-offs. • Villanova families enjoy all the technology, payment options, and information access conveniences that they expect from a first-rate institution.	• Develop the capacity of staff at all levels to utilize report generation and improve the use of in formation in decision-making. • Utilize management information to make better decisions, and improve recruitment, retention, and other sources of revenues.

Elements of VOI	Already Demonstrated	Potential/Targeted
Supporting business process reinvention and innovation	• Integration of "proven path" message through multiple channels, early in the student cycle. A single counseling contact point combines attributes of financial aid and student accounts.	• Early telephone outreach from the Counseling Center.
Increasing organizational competencies	• Education payment counselors are perceived by customers as value-added resources. More bills are paid on time, customers are happier, and vendors are almost transparent.	• Developing multi-year relationships between education payment counselors and the students/families they help.
Enabling collaboration and increasing capabilities	• Cross-departmental collaboration is enabled without infrastructure or budget barriers. Vendor alignment with institutional mission is being accomplished. Sharing best practices between TMS' partner institutions is enabled.	• Formalized best-practice benchmarking.
Enable new levels and kinds of leadership	• Institutional leadership is more focused on process-improvement, rather than transactional issues.	• Qualitative customer satisfaction measurements will be used for continuous improvement.

- The comprehensive financial assistance package to guide families in the development of payment solutions achieved a number of the institution's goals: payment plan participation increased by 33 percent over Villanova's previous plan, which attracted 1,800 participants (more than 2,400 students and families signed up in the first year). Interestingly, many families that previously borrowed or paid the tuition in full using credit cards decided to start earlier on a payment plan after receiving the clear marketing message. This increased Villanova's cash flow by approximately $500,000 in both June and July.

- In the first year of the partnership, the complete automatic life insurance coverage plan paid out over $30,000 to help students remain on campus and avoid write-offs at Villanova.

- Villanova had eliminated the use of credit cards for undergraduate student accounts. For families that insisted they needed to pay by credit card, Villanova implemented the TMS TuitionCharge service. TuitionCharge allows the institution to provide the convenience of credit cards through Tuition Management Systems. A convenience fee is charged per transaction by the system vendor and paid by the user. There is no merchant fee, which was previously absorbed by the institution. The smooth transition resulted in only a handful of families using this option as most were interested in mileage or rewards.

- A transition plan was jointly developed, enabling Villanova to maintain control over the solutions design and quality. Cross-departmental institutional feedback and suggestions resulted in a successful roll-out, customized for Villanova. A review process is ensuring consistency.

Demonstrable Outcomes

When considered in the context of the ROI discussion, positive tangible results were produced through the integrated education payment counseling model.

The VOI strategic pluses include a strong competitive advantage for the institution in several areas. From an enrollment management perspective, when students and families are given comprehensive financing solutions earlier in the cycle of admissions and financial aid packaging, the advantages are clear. As continuing students experience an integrated financial services environment on campus, the impact on satisfaction and retention is high.

As the university provides the strategic leadership of this innovative partnership, the professional staff can deliver comprehensive financial services to customers, and realize the intangible value of this approach.

What the Future Holds

Tuition Management Systems and Villanova University are embracing a best practices and continuous improvement approach to explore next stage options for tuition payment solutions. A critical consideration is to ensure that any steps taken result in an improved level of service and the development of a relationship with Villanova students and their families. Value added enhancements which continue to benefit the students and assist the university in meeting its financial objectives are integral to future developments. The objective is the creation of a positive feeling about Villanova that aligns with the institutional mission and helps build a lifetime relationship with students.

Evaluation of results across Villanova's campus communities and collaboration with other Villanova vendors and Tuition Management Systems' 700-plus partner institutions is being analyzed. Potential for the further integration and improvement of tuition payment solutions is being explored.

In its current state, the Web-based component of the counseling model is generic. Students must manually input their aid information in order to explore the best payment and financing options. TMS and Villanova wish to customize this service. The implementation of outbound, customized outreach counseling from the TMS Education Payment Counseling Center will be coordinated with Villanova's preferred lending partner to supplement the Villanova Financing Information Package, mailing, Web, campus point-of-contact and other channels and involves telephoning the bill payers for deposited, freshmen students. Done early in the planning process, it positively impacts the impression of Villanova affordability for the incoming students and is designed to proactively formalize their tuition payment planning.

In addition to improved student service, this customization will reduce institutional workload during busy summer periods, accelerates cash flow, and improves customer service.

Beyond business processing outsourcing, the TMS and Villanova experience demonstrates the power of a true resourcing relationship between two quality organizations with a commitment to higher education and a demonstrated focus on client service. By choosing resourcing, rather than outsourcing, Villanova has created a new competitive advantage for the institution.

National Student Clearinghouse Case Study

Case Study Abstract

The National Student Clearinghouse (NSC) is a non-profit organization founded 10 years ago by the higher education community. It is a powerful example of the principles embodied in the business value web. Deconstruction and reinvention of traditional linear business processes, coupled with advanced network and Web services technologies, will enable a new generation of many-party, multi-dimensional, services and process solutions. The NSC stands as the most exemplary case in higher education, providing an outstanding model and development history that foretells the changes underway in our solution delivery environment.

Founded in 1993 as the National Student Loan Clearinghouse, NSC provided a third-party solution to verification of enrollment, degrees, certificates, and transcripts for a wide range of financial intermediaries, employers, and other parties. By 2002, the records of 60 million students were handled through this enterprise. This service provides a substantial benefit to students, colleges and universities, and employers/insurers and has become a digital utility providing verification services. It is moving toward an any time, real time service model.

The NSC Case illustrates transitive trust, process deconstruction, and the deployment of Web services.

Addressing the Original Business Problem

NSC was created to solve a problem faced by all colleges and universities participating in the Guaranteed Student Loan Program, consisting of the Federal Family Education Loan Program (FFELP) and the National Direct Student Loan Program (Direct Lending). These programs shared a common business requirement with participating colleges and universities: ensuring that participants (lenders, government processors, guarantee agencies, and others) know when borrowers are in school, the status of their enrollment, and when they have ceased enrollment. What seems like a simple enough question, "Is the student still attending college?" becomes a very significant challenge when the numbers of GSL participants reaches in the millions of students, thousands of institutions, and hundreds of lenders and related program servicers.

This process is known as "enrollment verification." It began with early automated systems through a process of batch reports, mounds of computer printouts, and paper reporting. With some rudimentary technology progress in the early 1980s, participating financial institutions began exchanging magnetic tapes with colleges and universities, each asking the institutions to compare the listing of students on the banks' records with the registrars' enrollment records to determine the current status of enrollment. The matching, completed by approximately 800 lenders and 2,500 participating institutions, and covering several million student borrowers, was required to be executed three times each lending/enrollment cycle. Imagine the dozens of different formats used by lenders, the unique record layouts, status code variants, and the complexity of managing several lender relationships at each campus.

Mission Statement for National Student Clearinghouse.
The National Student Clearinghouse is the nation's largest source for post-secondary student degree and enrollment verification. Through its verification reporting solutions, NSC helps colleges and universities improve efficiency, reduce costs and workload, and enhance the quality-of-service they provide to their students and alumni, lending institutions, employers, and other organizations.

Inefficiency, inaccuracy, high costs, untimely reporting, and terrible customer service, coupled with increasing default problems, all led to a very simple and elegant solution that heralded a change that stands as a remarkable bellweather for what we see still coming in other areas today.

The National Student Clearinghouse leveraged its basic core competency into a variety of derivative business services.

Forming the Clearinghouse.

The industry participants came together and created the National Student Loan Clearinghouse in 1993, with each major GSL player contributing expertise, staffing support, board leadership, technology guidance, infrastructure, and financing. Colleges and universities were given the option of sending their enrollment information to one location, the clearinghouse, according to their reporting cycle, typically three times a semester, and the clearinghouse served as the trusted partner to share this information with the other participants in the loan program – lenders, guarantors, and servicers. While some institutions were reluctant to share this highly confidential and secure enrollment data with a third party, over time, they did.

By 2003, over 90 percent of the nations' enrollment records (representing 60 million students) were captured in what began as the National Student Loan Clearinghouse. Even if the story ended there, it would still be an important example of a collaborative and innovative industry solution to a challenging, data-intensive, transaction-based business problem.

New Name, New Solutions.

In the fall of 2000, however, quietly dropping the word "loan" from its name, the clearinghouse became The National Student Clearinghouse and began to develop several derivative business solutions for participating institutions. Today, the solutions include:

DegreeVerifysm – A process by which the NSC acts as the trusted proxy for the college or university to verify student degrees, certificates, and other educational achievements.

EnrollmentVerifysm – Relying upon data provided by the institutions, the NSC confirms enrollment for students who apply for student-based consumer services, credit instruments, travel discounts, health care insurance, tenant services, etc.

EnrollmentSearchsm – This service enables institutions to query the NSC's database to identify students' enrollment history and status at other institutions before, during, and after they have attended their institution.

TRA Reporting Service – Again relying on data already in its files, the NSC works with the schools' Hope/Lifetime Learning Tax Credit vendor to complete the Internal Revenue Service mandated 1098-T forms for students and the IRS.

LoanLocatorsm – This free Web-based service allows students themselves to quickly

National Student Clearinghouse

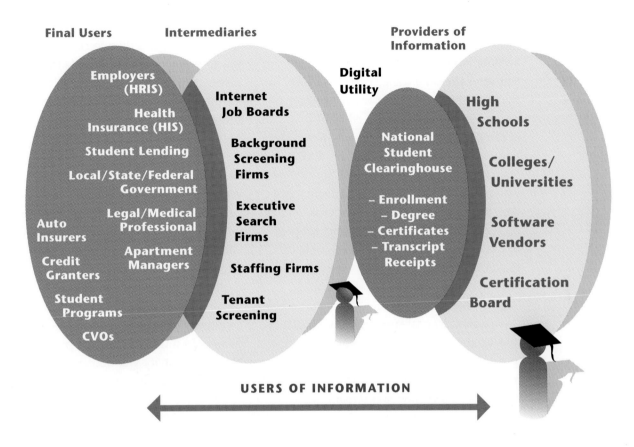

USERS OF INFORMATION

identify and locate their education loan holders. (As higher education institutions often sell the guaranteed loans on the secondary market, students can lose track of the lender who holds the loan, and for processing needs, consolidation loans, and other servicing issues, it often is useful to have a simple mechanism to "locate" all lenders.)

A Substantial Verification Service.
As of this writing, 2,700 colleges and universities participate in the enrollment verification service, representing 91 percent of the nation's enrollment, and the NSC performs more than 100 million verifications each year; 525 institutions participate in the Degree Verify service, representing 40 percent of the nation's degrees. These participation numbers continue to increase monthly, as more colleges and universities begin to see the value proposition of this service.

Chapter One discussed the use of BPO initiatives in the reinvention of core business processes. The processes of enrollment verification and degree verification are outstanding examples of critical functions that the campus must perform, and they meet Turk's test for a high level of importance. They are not functions or processes that will ever yield competitive advantage, however. They are also processes, that when outsourced to a provider such as the NSC, can be delivered with world-class service, significant cost savings, and a high quality of service and assured performance standard. The NSC represents a useful example of the successful business process outsourcing of a core process, one that is data and transaction intensive, with critical performance demands, and that can effectively be delivered by a trusted third party.

Digital utilities will become commonplace in higher education, providing dependable, low-cost, data transaction services. They will serve thousands of institutions.

New Technology Solutions

The technology infrastructure that enabled the initial development of the clearinghouse has advanced significantly. It now enables another important development that illustrates the significance of Web services in this evolution. The functions performed in the services described have all been accomplished through traditional file transfer exchange (FTP) processes and "batch" transmissions of records for verification. Using the recent advance of Web services technologies, standards, and protocols, the NSC is a pioneering adopter of the technology to move its business to a real-time processing mode. Mark Jones, NSC vice president of marketing and business development, recognizes that while there are many challenges in moving such a massive processing environment to this new technology, institutions, employers, and most importantly, students, are increasingly expecting and demanding a real time, any time, service solution.

Partnering with a Web Services-Savvy Solution Provider.

The NSC partnered with the Flamenco Network to manage the Web services-enabled version of its student enrollment and degree verification business. Flamenco will provide the management infrastructure and automate the Web services provisioning among the thousands of universities, businesses, and government organizations that may require verification of enrollment and degree data. Jones knew that they "would have major obstacles to overcome in implementing and managing a Web services project of this scope," so the clearinghouse focused on its core competencies and partnered with a company whose skills were in the network architecture and provisioning arena. While the NSC is processing over 100 million transactions per year, the clearinghouse expects that number to increase dramatically once the Web services interfaces are more widely available.

"We could have as many as 4,000 universities and over six million business and government organizations providing and requesting information, and each one of them represents a unique connection that has to be provisioned properly for the service to work," Jones says. Given the standards and protocols of Web services, this exceptional solution can be accomplished.

An Emergent Digital Utility.

We call this a "Digital Utility" – a comprehensive data exchange and networked solution that will provide high-volume data transaction services and integrated business process solutions for multiple trading partners, and all in a secure, real time, performance-based architecture that ensures consistent solution delivery in a trusted business partnership. The digital utility will become, we believe, a ubiquitous infrastructure solution component, not unlike the electrical, water, telephone, and other utilities we've come to expect to be present in our day-to-day lives. And as dependably as dial tone, we will increasingly expect these digital utilities to provide massive data transaction services in an instantaneous fashion, integrated with whatever business function we need, when we need them, and where we need them. The digital utility will find other application solution environments as businesses observe the pioneering success of solution providers such as the NSC, which touches so many business trading partners and consumers (students, employers, university student services providers, and lenders, to name a few).

Transitive Trust and Process Deconstruction Are Critical.

The NSC case illustrates "transitive trust," a concept fundamental to the potential of the business value web. Initially discussed by Gleason (2002) in the higher education and Web services context, transitive trust is a fundamental dimension of successful innovative and transformative business process reinvention. NSC's reinvention of the enrollment verification process illustrates the notion of "process deconstruction." What was once a linear, sequential business function involving two parties exchanging data to accomplish a process of enrollment verification, became a multi-party process with delegated or proxy authority given to an intermediary partner. In the initial solution, the lender went directly to the college or university with the request for enrollment status information; employers went directly to the campus for degree verification. With the introduction of the NSC model, a third party is introduced and vested with the trust to represent the trading partners in the transaction. Now, in the NSC case, this is a "simple" instance of a transaction brokered between two parties, but it does involve several key aspects of Gleason's notion of "transitive trust," which will be increasingly important to the development of future networked business solutions.

To truly begin to take advantage of the Web services potential, to open the door to fundamental business process innovation, and to realize increasing value in new process models, a foundation in transitive trust must be built. Gleason originally discussed transitive trust in the context of the developing infrastructure of digital security and public key infrastructure (PKI) and Internet transaction authentication schemas. It extends to any complex business transaction, however, and is as simple as assigning responsibility for identification, authentication, and authorization of the parties to the transaction, and the trusted agents are vested with their proxy's authority. Transitive trust will become key. Without it, the emergence of the business value web model would not occur.

Transitive trust is a necessary ingredient for the emergence of the array of business value web applications and solutions.

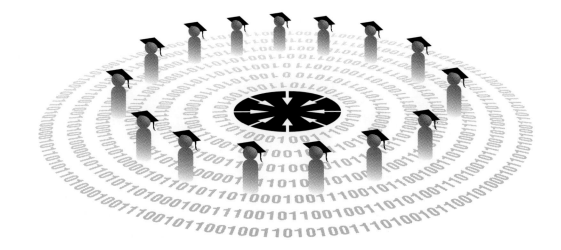

Demonstrable Outcomes

In terms of our discussion of ROI and VOI, the NSC case offers some interesting results and instances of the power of the digital utility to derive both ROI and VOI. This table captures some high-level observations.

Demonstrable Outcomes of the NSC Case

Elements of ROI	Already Demonstrated	Potential/Targeted
Reduced Cost	• Higher education institutions and trading partners save on processing costs through economies of scale. • Increased speed to solution reduces wait time on other processes and produces a gain in efficiency. • Trading partners absorb costs of the transaction. (Institutions do not pay a transaction fee – the lenders or employers cover these costs.)	• Additional verification functions to be considered for outsourcing. • Staff reallocation possible to other less clerical processes.
Measurable Service Improvements	• Students are much more satisfied with customer service levels and real time resolution of transaction. • Will grow to over 90 percent of nation's enrollment in 10 years, representing 100 million transactions annually.	• New processes will also improve customer satisfaction. • Development is continuation of "derivative" service solutions based on existing network and transaction services.

Elements of VOI	Already Demonstrated	Potential/Targeted
Increased Market Opportunity	• Jones estimates that the NSC made back its initial $25,000 investment in Web services from new revenue from its existing largest 25 customers in the first month of operations of the Web services solution set.	• Jones believes Web service application offers potential for doubling market size.
Support Reinvention and Innovation	• The enrollment verification process has been transformed, as has degree verification.	• This demonstrates great opportunity for many other processes to be reinvented.
Enable Collaboration	• Multiple parties come together in a collaborative, trusted relationship to solve shared business problems.	• Other trading partners will be identified to join clearinghouse community.

University of Pennsylvania/Affiliated Computer Services Case Study

Case Study Abstract

The University of Pennsylvania is a national leader in creative outsourcing arrangements. In 1997, the university was seeking to change the way it serviced financial aid on campus. The goal was a one-stop shop in student financial servicing in order to improve services while reducing administrative costs. Penn selected Affiliated Computer Services' outsourcing solutions.

Affiliated Computer Services (ACS) acquired AFSA Data Corporation in 2002, dramatically increasing its involvement in higher education. Combined, the companies service FFELP, Perkins, and Direct loans for more than eight million borrowers.

In addition, ACS provides a suite of cutting-edge administrative products and services for campuses nationwide. These outsourcing solutions include a suite of integrated, Web-based products and services designed to ease the administrative burden for higher education instiutions, while facilitating access for students and their families. ACS's strategic intent is to develop BPO solutions in seven verticals in higher education: admissions/recruiting, alumni relations/development, student services, academic information services, financial services, IT services, and administrative and other.

Mission Statement for University of Pennsylvania:
Founded in Philadelphia in 1757 by Benjamin Franklin, Penn is one of the world's leading research universities.

Business Process Outsourcing in Higher Education

ACS is a $4 billion organization serving a broad cross-section of commercial clients, state and local government clients, and federal government clients. With its acquisition of AFSA Data Corporation, it also serves higher education. ACS helps large organizations restructure business processes and costs so that they can reinvest in their core products. BPO is business process outsourcing. It's 70 percent of ACS's business and is growing rapidly, in both the commercial and the government sectors. BPO is, very simply, the outsourcing of mission-critical non-core business processes. These processes are prerequisites to achieving excellence in core operations but are not competitive differentiators to an organization. Some enterprises get so bogged down in the day-to-day back office operations that they lose focus on their core products, services, and clients. ACS's BPO services let its clients focus on what's important.

BPO in Education Is Poised for Growth.
In education, services outsourcing focuses on non-critical and non-core functions, such as food services, bookstore, and the like. BPO focuses on critical but non-core functions such as financial services, academic information services, and alumni relations/development. While the state of BPO development in education is lagging behind that of government and commercial sectors, it is expected to gain.

BPO is a natural evolution of information technology outsourcing – the other 30 percent of ACS's business. ACS oversees information technology operations for clients through management of data centers, complex communication networks, software and other functions that support information technology. The more time ACS spent consolidating IT operations, the more it realized the real opportunity was to attack the entire process. Technology is always an integral component of BPO.

Outsourcing in Higher Education

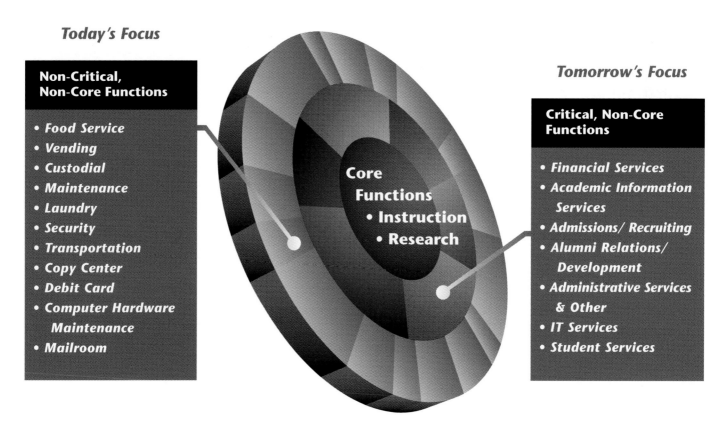

Today's Focus

Non-Critical, Non-Core Functions

- *Food Service*
- *Vending*
- *Custodial*
- *Maintenance*
- *Laundry*
- *Security*
- *Transportation*
- *Copy Center*
- *Debit Card*
- *Computer Hardware Maintenance*
- *Mailroom*

Core Functions
- **Instruction**
- **Research**

Tomorrow's Focus

Critical, Non-Core Functions

- *Financial Services*
- *Academic Information Services*
- *Admissions/ Recruiting*
- *Alumni Relations/ Development*
- *Administrative Services & Other*
- *IT Services*
- *Student Services*

Outsourcing Solutions in Seven Verticals in Higher Education.
BPO encompasses virtually every back office process that supports the core mission of an organization. The processes have a few characteristics in common: they are mission critical, information intensive, and labor intensive. They also are expensive processes processes where BPO can achieve economies of scale through the effective use of technology. BPO solutions have been or will be developed for many of the processes in the seven vertical areas portrayed in the figure on this page.

ACS BPO services yield both process improvement and reduced costs. The process improvements flow from the use of advanced technology, centralization, and process simplification. Cost savings are realized through labor rate arbitrage and economies of scale, achieved through facilities management or shared services.

The shared services delivery model leverages people, processes, and technology to provide the benefits of a world-class infrastructure without the capital outlay and cost structure required for maintaining in-house operations. Shared services uses concentric layers of common infrastructure (facilities, technology, and operations management), common transactional services, and common industry services to support a final ring of client-specific services (see figure on page 9).

ACS is deeply involved in helping make college accessible to millions of families through its roles: 1) supporting the delivery of financial aid – FAFSA processing, Pell Grant processing, delivery and servicing of loans in all three federal student loan programs (FFEL, Direct, and Perkins); and 2) providing financial aid outsourcing services to institutions such as the University of Phoenix.

Seven Verticals for Critical but Non-Core Functions

Admissions/ Recruiting

- *Marketing*
- *Admissions Apps.*
- *Enrollment Mgmt.*

Alumni Relations Development

- *Fundraising*
- *Community*
- *Telemarketing*
- *Direct Mail*

Administrative & Other

- *Human Resources*
- *Cash Management*
- *Auxiliary Services*

Student Services

- *Account Mgmt.*
- *Career Counseling*
- *Campus Life*
- *Foreign Student Services*

Academic Information Services

- *Grades*
- *Registration*
- *Catalog*
- *Transcripts*
- *Degree Verification*
- *Degree Audit*
- *Degree Advisement*

Financial Services

- *Financial Planning*
- *Financial Aid Apps.*
- *Financial Aid Packaging*
- *Award & Fulfillment*
- *Debt Organization*
- *Debt Servicing*
- *A/R & Debt Receivables*
- *Debt Collection*
- *Tax & Financial Reporting*

IT Services

- *Network Support*
- *Data Center*
- *Development*
- *Web Site*
- *Platform Maintenance*

| Call Center | Mail Fulfillment | Payment Processing | Records Management |

Major Cross-Functional Processes

Times have changed significantly in the past three years. If colleges and universities are to be successful in the future they need to deliver high-quality service, with integrity, at a low cost. This means that all must focus on what they do best. Colleges and universities must deliver high quality education, lenders must deliver low cost capital, and companies such as ACS must continually deliver higher-quality services at a lower cost.

The University of Pennsylvania

The University of Pennsylvania is a leading research university. It has been one of the national leaders in creative outsourcing arrangements. ACS has provided student loan management services for Penn for more than 30 years.

ACS Solutions Currently Provided to Penn. In 1997, the university was seeking to change the way it serviced financial aid on campus. Penn desired a one-stop shop in student financial servicing in order to improve services while reducing administrative costs.

Mission Statement for Affiliated Computer Services:
ACS is involved in a growing variety of business process outsourcing services for colleges, universities, lenders, secondary markets, and many others involved in educating America's youth.

Penn selected ACS to help business and financial aid personnel manage institutional loan portfolios, default rates, and receivables.

ACS created a special file for receiving tuition receivables from the university and customized programs to load data into the ACS system and retain complete history of the accounts from Penn's system. ACS' new collection manager system also supports this process. ACS dedicates staff to Penn in support of the university's "Default Prevention Program."

The university offers a private loan program that ACS has serviced. When the university began offering the Wharton Loan Program in 1999, ACS developed special programs and procedures to support it. ACS works closely with the university on default prevention and offers special payment arrangements to borrowers to reduce loan defaults. Focused cure measures are initiated for defaulted accounts in an effort to give borrowers an opportunity to repay their loans.

ACS also provides 1098-T reporting services for the university for Hope Scholarship and Lifetime Learning through the Tax Credit Reporting Service (TCRS). This gives the university the technology and tools it needs to meet new and existing IRS tax credit-reporting requirements.

Tax year 2003 was the last waiver year in which higher education institutions were exempt from reporting financial information on 1098-T forms. All colleges and universities are required to begin reporting financial information for tax year 2004.

TCRS also provides students and parent taxpayers with detailed financial information, organized to assist them in claiming available tax credits. TCRS is a comprehensive set of services designed to help institutions, students, and their parents take advantage of available tax credits.

Benefits Achieved

Partnering with ACS for BPO has allowed Penn to reorganize its internal operations to assure that staff are used in the capacities where they are most needed. Penn transferred the cost- and time-intensive staff transactions to ACS, which allows the staff to focus more on student services.

The university entrusted control of its student loan programs to ACS, which has resulted in significant reductions in default rates and lowered administrative costs.

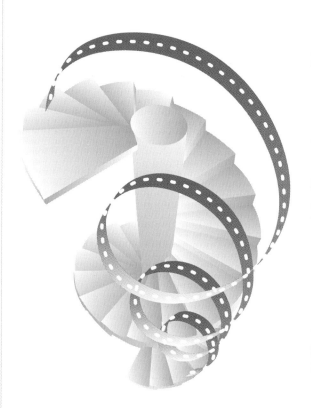

The George Washington University/BearingPoint Case Study

Case Study Abstract

BearingPoint has worked with The George Washington University over a 15-year relationship, providing many services and solutions. GW is the largest university in the nation's capital, with enrollments of more than 20,000 and a wide range of programs at the undergraduate, graduate, and professional levels, including a medical center.

BearingPoint is a global business advisor and systems integrator. Two decades ago, it became one of the first major companies to designate a specific vertical practice for providing technology and management consulting services to higher education. BearingPoint seeks to provide its clients with an accelerated ROI through process improvements, cost reductions, and productivity gains. Today, the firm serves more than 50 colleges and universities around the United States.

Recently, GW and BearingPoint completed three Web services applications that enhanced the university's data services to students, faculty and other stakeholders. These included: 1) improved accounting and financial reporting, 2) a data warehouse and executive information system, and 3) an e-workforce initiative. This case study illustrates the sorts of expert services and business process reinventions that are part of today's relationships between universities and solutions partners.

Leveraging Web Services at The George Washington University

Founded in 1821 and chartered by the United States Congress, The George Washington University (GW) is the largest higher education institution in the nation's capital. Its nine major schools offer hundreds of undergraduate, graduate, and professional programs. Each year, the university enrolls a diverse population of 20,500 undergraduate, graduate, and professional students from all 50 states, the District of Columbia, and more than 140 countries.

GW recognizes the importance of providing students, faculty, staff, and alumni with best-in-class, user-friendly services. To help strengthen GW's relationships with these key stakeholders, BearingPoint was engaged to assist with GW's Web services projects. The choice was based on the company's 15-year record of delivering successful projects across the GW organization, its higher education experience, and its ability to provide guidance on issues of strategy as well as technology.

With BearingPoint's assistance, GW sought to strengthen its online capabilities with three Web services projects: 1) improved financial accounting/reporting for system users, 2) data warehouse and executive information system, and 3) e-workforce.

George Washington University's mission statement describes "a student-focused community… built upon a foundation of integrity, creativity, and openness to the exploration of new ideas." In this context, GW strives for continuous process improvement that supports the highest-quality service delivery. Recently, BearingPoint assisted the university with several Web services projects that leverage online capabilities to optimize business processes and elevate service levels in key areas.

"One reason we've ramped up our relationship is because we decided we want to tap into their strategic thinking across the board, not just on specific projects. We want to rebuild our university to make it more efficient, friendly, and productive. Doing so involves not just technology, but processes. Knowing the best practices and where technology plays a role, and tying it all together, is critical—that's what they do. We want to be on the leading edge, and BearingPoint is our strategic partner to get us there."

David Swartz, Chief Information Officer, George Washington University

The data warehouse and executive information capabilities are an excellent example of how basic ERP systems and other legacy systems can be enhanced by Web services applications.

Improved Accounting and Financial Reporting for System Users.

With the university's existing, mainframe-based system, users processed and reviewed significant amounts of paperwork while receiving little useful information in return. Many departments created expensive stand-alone financial systems to generate the needed information. After reviewing several enterprise resource planning offerings, GW decided to replace its existing systems with Oracle's Financial Management application, which would provide a project accounting module specifically designed to accommodate university research as well as a Web-based application architecture. BearingPoint provided end-to-end support during this project. For example, the company helped GW:

- develop a detailed capacity and implementation plan;

- leverage technical and functional support throughout the implementation;

- supplement Oracle's application implementation methodology with change management and conference room pilot tasks and deliverables; and

- transition employees to Oracle modules including General Ledger, Accounts Payable, Purchasing, Grants Management/ Projects, Inventory, and Accounts Receivable

As a result, GW users benefit from faster and more effective data processing and reporting through streamlined workflows. Improved access to timely and relevant information via a Web browser has enhanced the ability of stakeholders to make Informed decisions. Stand-alone systems have been eliminated.

The Student Data Mart (SDM)

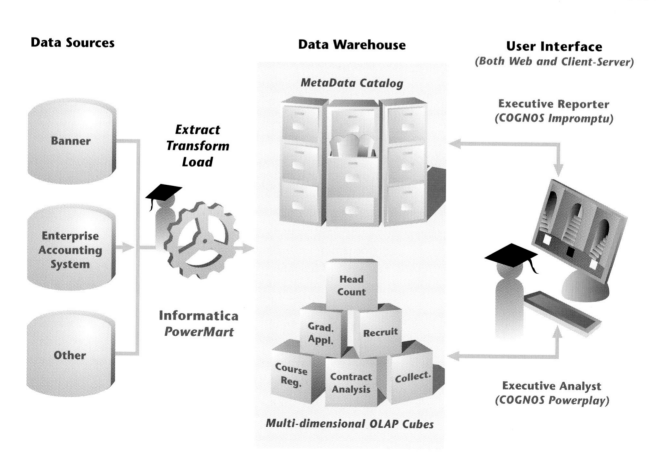

Data Sources

Banner

Enterprise Accounting System

Other

Extract Transform Load

Informatica PowerMart

Data Warehouse

MetaData Catalog

Head Count

Grad. Appl.

Recruit

Course Reg.

Contract Analysis

Collect.

Multi-dimensional OLAP Cubes

User Interface
(Both Web and Client-Server)

Executive Reporter
(COGNOS Impromptu)

Executive Analyst
(COGNOS Powerplay)

Data Warehouse and Executive Information Services.

GW's users were not satisfied with the data and analytic capabilities offered by Banner's On-line Transactional Processing (OLTP) system.

The Student Data Mart (SDM) uses the latest data warehousing methodology. The main goal for SDM is to allow more users to access student demographic and academic information in a user-friendly and self-service manner, giving people the opportunity to analyze the entire student lifecycle at GW with information available at their fingertips. The Student Account Data Mart (SADM) is implemented and integrated with SDM. It provides reporting and analytical features to Student Accounts Receivable personnel so that a comprehensive accounts view can be accessed easily in a timely manner.

The benefits of the student data mart are clear:

1. Users can access information directly over the Intranet, drawing from a clean repository with powerful reporting tools.
2. The integration of SDM processes and reports has exposed many data quality issues resulting from distributed data ownership, and undertaken resolution.
3. Reusable reports, generated by the user and available for sharing with others, are enabling movement from an environment of expensive, "one-off" reports to a "publish-and-subscribe" paradigm.
4. This may lead eventually to an enterprise-wide data warehouse for GW.

"It would be an understatement to say that the Cognos cubes were extremely useful... I would like to express my appreciation, as well of those of my colleagues who are Cognos users, for the professionalism and adherence to the principles of TQM by the staff of Data Administration."

Dr. Norayr Katcheressian, Associate Dean Columbian School of Arts and Sciences

E-Workforce.

GW needs to get more productivity out of its employees, control costs, and enhance customer services. To achieve these ends, GW needs to attract, develop, and recognize a new generation of highly motivated employees. GW has created an employee-focused core group, comprised of personnel from different areas of the university. BearingPoint Inc. is working with the university and the employee-focused core group to address the above issues and to implement innovative approaches to delivering services. These will enable employees and managers to perform everyday activities themselves, anytime and anywhere.

The core group is working toward creating an employee service model. This will allow for a structure in which transactional and operational functions are integrated in the business units across the university. The resulting service integration and "one stop shopping" for employees will be achieved through a service contact center, providing an informative and user friendly Web site, offering self-service options, and monitoring real-time performance at the various stages of the employee's life cycle. The group has developed a list of recommended projects and activities that are being undertaken, with BearingPoint's assistance.

Demonstrable Outcomes.

These three Web service applications have already yielded clear returns on the investment, with even more substantial returns possible over time. Moreover, these initiatives have demonstrated the first wave of VOI, with more substantial elements to come.

"...this is exactly what we had been promised would come with Banner ...and I doubt that anyone realistically thought that it would ever arrive. It certainly seems we were wrong!"

Phillip Wirtz, Professor of Management Science, School of Business and Public Management

"From my point of view, the Data Mart has been a labor-saver!"

Clint Williams, Assistant Director, Graduate Student Enrollment Management

Demonstrable Outcomes of the BearingPoint Case

Elements of ROI	Already Demonstrated	Potential/Targeted
Reduced Costs for Families	• *Eliminate stand-alone financial systems.* • *Improve workflow, process flow.* • *Reduce cost of report generation.*	• *Aggressively improve workflow and performance of financial and accounting systems.* • *Further reduce costs of information generation and deployment of special reports.*
Enhanced Services, Increases in Revenues	• *Enhance financial reporting, improved workflow.* • *Access to executive and management information that was never before available.*	• *Develop the capacity of staff at all levels to utilize report generation and improve the use of information in decision-making.* • *Utilize management information to make better decisions, improve recruitment, retention, and other sources of revenues.*

Elements and Nature of VOI	Already Demonstrated	Potential/Targeted
1. Enable new levels and kinds of leadership		• *Better information will support and enhance decision-making and leadership at all levels.*
2. Support reinvention and innovation		• *Better information will support a variety of process and service improvements.*
3. Formalize knowledge management and make better use of knowledge	• *Create a utility for accessing, analyzing and reporting on student and student accounts data.*	• *May lead to creation of a true, enterprise-wide data mart.*
4. Enable collaboration and use of communities of practice		• *Availability of information will support the development of working groups and communities of practice.*
5. Increase individual and organizational competencies		• *Staff at all levels will have the capacity to develop and utilize the information they need.*
Nature of VOI: Organizational Impact, Scope, and Dynamics	• *Scope – Initially tactical* • *Organizational Impact – Enhance individual performance, achieve competitive parity* • *Dynamics – initially productivity enhancement*	• *Scope – potentially strategic* • *Organizational impact – potentially establish competitive advantage* • *Dynamics – potentially build on productivity enhancement to yield collaboration and innovation*

Insights About Value from the Case Studies

The case studies provide six different perspectives on how to realize VOI in real-life situations. None of these enterprises began their initiatives with the clearly articulated goal of maximizing value from their business processes and solutions. Yet the framework of value/ROI/VOI proved to be a useful lens through which to analyze the impacts of these initiatives on enhancing value for these different enterprises. Moreover, enhancing value provides a unifying theme that links the different kinds of initiatives, from enterprise-wide efforts like those at The Boston Consortium and Loyola Marymount initiatives to targeted, "point" solutions like tuition management at Villanova University or receivables management services at the University of Pennsylvania or Web service applications at The George Washington University.

The following series of observations emerge from these six cases. These can be helpful to higher education leadership in accelerating the understanding and development of VOI.

Access to New Technology and Human Resources Is Critical to Enhancing Value

Achieving enhancements in value requires institutions to access both new technology and human resources capacities, either through investment or partnership. All of the case studies relied on new information and communication technology capabilities to varying degrees. Some were realized through new development of institutional infrastructure, while others relied on resourcing arrangements with solution providers. Technology was necessary, but not sufficient.

The nurturing of human infrastructures and competencies was the centerpiece of The Boston Consortium case. The acquisition of enterprise-wide IT competencies was a keystone of the Collegis arrangement with Loyola Marymount. Human resources were key ingredients in all the other cases, as well, although not at an enterprise-level like at The Boston Consortium and Loyola Marymount University.

Both technology and human infrastructures and capacities are fundamental to building value. However, competencies in innovation and process reinvention at the institutional level require longer development time. They are also more difficult. It has taken The Boston Consortium several years to build a human development framework and culture that is now poised to achieve truly significant VOI. Institutions like Loyola Marymount and Valencia Community College require two or three years to begin to reap significant VOI from resourcing technology. Moreover, experience has shown it often takes three years into an ERP implementation for process reinvention to yield significant dividends, and the process can proceed for four or five more years beyond that. It takes time for technology and human resources infrastructures to come together in a way that they can support process reinvention and innovation.

Investment in technology and human resources infrastructures must go hand-in-hand for institutions to build value. These investments take time to develop and must be held to high expectations.

Most institutions cannot afford the luxury of investing in technology without making a serious commitment to process reinvention and innovation in institutional dynamics.

Innovation and Process Reinvention Are the Heart of VOI

Meaningful VOI cannot be achieved without innovation in organizational dynamics and process reinvention. This is demonstrated by all the cases. Substantial VOI was achieved by process reinvention, either by the institutions or by solution providers. This is why it is misleading to attempt to predict the ultimate VOI from a major technology infrastructure investment, such as the development of an enterprise network, implementation of a new ERP suite, or portalization of the institution's back-office operations. The VOI in these efforts will emerge over time as processes are reinvented. Such VOI will depend on the level of institutional commitment, will, skill, and capacity. These elements are unknown and perhaps unknowable at the planning stage.

However, VOI has a powerful role to play when an institution is contemplating a major investment such as ERP. VOI should raise the bar for the level of process reinvention that the institutional leadership and grassroots users should expect. It should shape institutional plans. Today, most institutions considering a major ERP investment should not undertake that investment unless they are willing to commit to pervasive and continuous reinvention. At the front end of the selection process, equivalent energy should be invested in preparing the campus community for resourcing and reinvention as in evaluating the qualifications of the solutions providers.

Institutional leadership needs to tell the story of building value and develop the capacity of grassroots leaders to do the same.

On the other hand, institutional leadership can predict value from investment and changes in resourcing arrangements for particular business processes and solutions. Many resourcing solutions providers have both the experience and metrics to assist in this effort. Targeting the levels of ROI and VOI expected from enhancements to particular business processes is an important element of the resourcing decision.

Impactful Innovations Utilize Multiple Elements of VOI

One can deconstruct the elements of VOI in particular institutional processes and initiatives. This is useful in understanding what those elements are and how they fit together. However, most institutional initiatives deal with multiple elements of VOI. The most powerful initiatives leverage the synergy between the different elements, especially those developing human capital and the capacity to collaborate and innovate. The Boston Consortium, for example, uses strong leadership, collaboration, and development of human capital to create the environment for successful reinvention initiatives. This releases grassroots leadership and innovative energies. The level of success of business process outsourcing initiatives such as Tuition Management Systems and Affiliated Computer Sservices and Web services solutions such as BearingPoint depends on the solution providers' experience and skill in leveraging these multiple elements of VOI.

The colleges and universities in the case studies have significant potential for great VOI in the future. This will be achieved in a variety of ways, including leveraging multiple elements of VOI.

"Point" Solutions Are a Key Element of Value Building

One of the advantages in business process outsourcing and Web services-based "point solutions" is that the solutions partners have already developed the technology and human resources needed for value-building solutions. As the development of Web services advances, institutional leadership will have the option to evaluate many point solutions for potential integration into their portfolio of business process resourcing decisions. They will also be able to consider new ways of leveraging these reinvented processes to create previously untapped sources of value for college and university stakeholders.

John Seely Brown refers to the power of accumulated process enhancements and reinventions as *radical incrementalism* (2003). Transformative innovations are more likely to emerge from a host of continuously expeditionary initiatives, spanning the institution, than from a few planned, large-scale change efforts.

One of the strengths of these point solutions is that the VOI results are focused and relatively easy to measure. The insights on how to enhance VOI in a number of processes can be used to stimulate resourcing and reinvention decisions in a broad range of institutional processes. Institutions like the University of Pennsylvania have experimented with outsourcing and resourcing initiatives in a broad range of administrative and academic support areas.

Value Building Is a Mixture of Strategic and Tactical Actions

Strategic vision, decisions, and commitments are necessary to build the technology and human infrastructures essential to building value. They are also necessary to change institutional culture, deconstruct existing processes and practices, and provide the catalyst for process reinvention. These strategic actions were clearly visible in the Boston Consortium and Collegis cases, and formed a backdrop for the other cases. Strategic visions and actions set the stage for the myriad tactical decisions that are necessary to build value through continuous, incremental innovation, reinvention, and improvement.

Enterprises Need to Articulate the Importance of Optimizing Value

Colleges and universities need unifying themes to understand and focus their investments in infrastructure, human development, and innovation. Enhancing value and achieving VOI are powerful metaphors that can be useful to institutions in articulating the strategic and tactical goals of innovation. Efforts like the Boston Consortium's use of Learning Histories to memorialize insights should also use the concept of value building to engage the campus community in applying these concepts.

The case studies validate the potential for using the concepts of enhancing value and resourcing business processes to advance institutional service to stakeholders and competitiveness.

Decision Processes Supported by VOI

Three essential decision processes can use the concept of enhancing value and VOI to illuminate alternatives, stimulate measurement and monitoring of progress, and establish stretch goals. The following table suggests how the case studies validated the potential for VOI to support such decision processes.

The case studies capture today's state-of-the-art in resourcing. Although not expressly using ROI/VOI, most of the institutions and solutions providers involved in the cases had developed their own set of metrics and vocabulary that anticipated the ROI/VOI formulation. Some of the case study participants have started to use the concepts of value and ROI/VOI to describe their efforts. The following chapter explores how colleges and universities can deploy these concepts through resourcing.

VOI's Potential to Support Decision Processes

Decision Processes	*Actions and Use of VOI*	*Case Study Examples*
Development of Enterprise Technology and Human Resources Infrastructure	• *Develop technology and infrastructure as a strategic investment, building the capacity to innovate and reinvent processes.* • *Use VOI to set stretch goals.*	• *Boston Consortium built human resources development infrastructure. High expectations, few specific measures for enterprise-wide results.* • *Loyola Marymount established a strategic relationship to provide IT infrastructure and outsourced competencies. Specific performance indicators are part of resourcing agreement.* • *Technology infrastructure and human resource competencies in particular process areas acquired through BPO and point solutions at Villanova, Penn, and George Washington.* • *In the future, specific stretch goals using VOI could be deployed to support decisions on technology and human resource investments.*
Resourcing the Portfolio of Business Processes	• *Orchestrate resourcing decisions in the portfolio of processes using VOI.* • *Focus on point solutions for particular processes, establish performance measures for processes.*	• *All cases used metrics and expectations of performance for specific processes or initiatives.* • *These measures can be strengthened and extended to reflect ROI/VOI principles.*
Strategic Reaction to the Economic Environment	• *Continuous attention to enhancing quality and controlling costs, at all levels, as part of a comprehensive effort to improve institutional competitive position and enhance the value proposition.*	• *Boston Consortium was founded to enhance quality and control costs, across all functions and institutions.* • *All institutions in the cases can leverage their resourcing efforts to be a part of a comprehensive institutional effort to enhance their value proposition.*

CHAPTER 4

Future Tools, Responsibilities, and Improving Resourcing Decisions

- *Future Tools: Web Services, Open Source, Loosely Coupled Applications*
- *From Value Chain to Business Value Web*
- *The Business Officer's Emerging Responsibilities*
- *10 Initiatives to Improve Resourcing Decisions*
- *Vignette from the Future*
- *Leadership, Innovation, and Reinvention*

This chapter takes a glimpse at the future of resourcing. The development of the business value web will be accelerated over the next few years by the deployment of a new arsenal of applications based on three concepts: Web services, open source, and loosely coupled/tightly integrated solutions. These will enable the development of highly targeted, best-of-breed applications that can be seamlessly stitched into the institutional business value web. Digital utilities such as the National Student Clearinghouse will proliferate, including leading-edge institutions offering best-of-breed solutions to other institutions and even greater marketplaces.

In many institutions, the business officer is uniquely positioned to understand how the pieces of the business process portfolio fit together, and how they contribute to value. At the strategic level, business officers will shape and inform executive decisions on the institution's portfolio of business processes. In addition, the business officer will orchestrate the continuous churning of resourcing decisions relating to the individual elements of the process portfolio. The business officer will also play a key role in IT decisions relating to business processes, if such processes are to be successful.

This chapter includes an interconnected set of 10 parallel initiatives that business officers should undertake to advance the state of resourcing decisions on their campus. It concludes with a vignette from the future, describing the potential role of a business officer in orchestrating the optimization of the business value web.

Terms and Concepts

Authentication: The process of authenticating the identity of a user in a portal or Web services application.

Digital Rights Management/Digital Asset Management: Enterprises develop the policies, protocols, and infrastructures needed to manage, meter, and exchange their knowledge.

Digital Certificates: Certification of the veracity of digital information.

Digital Signatures. In a digital setting, today's broad legal concept of "signature" may well include markings as diverse as digitized images of paper signatures, typed notations such as "/s/ John Smith," or even addressing notations, such as electronic mail origination headers. See http://www.abanet.org/scitech/ec/isc/dsg-tutorial.html.

e-Knowledge: Digital representations of content and context become e-knowledge through the dynamics of human engagement with them. E-knowledge also represents the fusion of e-learning and knowledge management.

Interoperability: The ability of data, applications, and platforms to communicate with one another.

Loosely Coupled: Loosely coupled is an attribute of systems, referring to an approach to designing interfaces across modules to reduce the interdependencies across modules, or components – in particular, reducing the risk that changes within one module will create unanticipated changes within other modules. This approach specifically seeks to increase flexibility in adding modules, replacing modules and changing operations within individual modules.

Open Source: Applications and devices whose source codes are known and operate according to open standards and are in the public domain as "shareware," free of license fees.

Public Key Infrastructure (PKI): PKI and digital certificate solutions used by enterprises, Web sites, and consumers to conduct secure communications and transactions over the Internet and private networks.

SOAP: Simple Object Access Protocol is a messaging standard or protocol to allow Internet applications to communicate.

Tightly Coupled: Traditional application systems are integrated through "hard programming" in a tightly coupled manner that makes integration and modification difficult.

UDDI: Universal Description, Discovery and Integration is a Web directory that allows applications to announce the availability and services to other applications. UDDI is the white pages and yellow pages of Web services.

WSDL: Web Services Description Language is an XML format used to describe the capabilities and interoperability required of a Web service.

XML: Extensible Markup Language uses tags to describe how a document or knowledge object will be used. While HTML is used to describe how a document will be displayed on a browser, XML describes how programs and/or knowledge objects can be processed by a program, an application, or a system.

Future Tools: Web Services, Open Source, Loosely Coupled Applications

A new generation of tools, techniques, and practices will make it easier to deconstruct and reinvent business processes, using loosely coupled software applications. This will increase the number and nature of resourcing options and tap the latent richness of the business value web.

Web Services

Many experts predict an increase in the adoption of Web services technology in higher education, just as the services are advancing in other sectors. More and more business applications will move to the new standards and protocols that ground Web service technologies. We anticipate that this will lead to significant changes in the delivery of many core administrative functions on campuses. As Carl Jacobsen, chief information officer at the University of Delaware, argued persuasively,

> *"...the promise of Web services lies in its ability to resolve the differences among shared, networked applications. Applications from different vendors, of various vintages, written in different languages, running on disparate platforms, easily communicate and cooperate, resolving their differences to act in concert."*
>
> *(EDUCAUSE Review, April 2002)*

Imagine the world of administrative systems on our campuses when we truly can easily link disparate systems with each other through the standards and protocols of Web services. Business processes, which we have argued will undergo a process of deconstruction and innovation, will be freed from their hard-wired current ties to existing systems and technologies. With the freedom of an information systems architecture built upon Web services technology, powerful transformation will be possible.

Web services are just an instrument, however. The cultural change enabled by the technology advances lies at the center of the transformation opportunity. We believe it is the role of the business officer to help provide the leadership for the transformation, in partnership with the information technology professionals on campus.

As Jacobsen suggests, we have the opportunity to leverage existing legacy software systems, and the campus does not have to "rip and replace" old applications in many cases. The technology exists to code interfaces and Web services modules that can "loosely couple" older software programs that have served the campus well for many years. With Web services protocols and interoperable interfaces written, component legacy applications can in fact be "saved" and work well in a new configuration with Web services "wrappers." These newly updated components can in fact work well with other systems on campus and those external to the campus suite of systems, in an effective and efficient design architecture based upon the emerging Web services standards.

Web services hold great promise as a tool for future development, as validated by the commitment of significant development resources by Microsoft, IBM, Sun, and other major information systems and services providers. Such investments will likely help campus leaders realize the potential of the business value web. Examples of web services applications in higher education include the National Student Clearinghouse and BearingPoint cases.

"For colleges and universities, implementation of Web services can translate into increased efficiencies, improved customer services, and institution-wide resource savings."

Bernard W. Gleason

"The loosely coupled architectures enabled by Web Services technologies start with the assumption that robustness – the ability to perform in highly complex and uncertain environments – requires greater flexibility."

John Seely Brown

Loosely Coupled/Tightly Coupled

Business enterprises are a cycle ahead of higher education in deploying Web services to create competitive advantage and leveraged growth. In *Out of the Box*, John Hagel III provides a powerful description of how innovative enterprises are using Web services to reinvent their business processes, reduce costs, and leverage their growth, often penetrating into previously unreachable new markets. These are valuable lessons for colleges and universities grappling with "Tough Times, Big Choices."

The table below illustrates how loosely coupled applications and services change the roles, rules, approaches to renewal, and benefits of business processes. In higher education, many of the attempts at process reinvention in the 1990s used tightly coupled approaches that "hardwired" the solutions, creating inflexible fixes that failed the test of time. In the future, process reinvention will shift from tightly coupled/hardwired solutions to loosely coupled, tightly integrated solutions.

Open Source

Open source initiatives demonstrate a dramatic advancement in our systems development evolution, heralding tremendous potential for the higher education community. Consider the demonstrable success of the widely adopted "uPortal" initiative, through which powerful Web portal solutions have been built by the higher education community, for the community, with advanced, state-of-the-art technology and standards as a foundation. Hundreds of colleges and universities are adopting the uPortal system as their campus portal technology solution, as are some important corporate partners (Campus Pipeline, for example), paying no software license fees. Campus systems professionals have sought the uPortal solution because it provides state-of-the-art technology, developed by and for the campus community, meeting the best practice functional standards requirements of the community. Additionally, the economics of the open source business model make for a compelling case in these times of economic strain.

Contrasting Tightly and Loosely Coupled Applications

	Tightly Coupled	Loosely Coupled
Business Process Roles	• *Controller* • *Limited, all-purpose service providers*	• *Orchestrator* • *Increasingly specialized service providers*
Business Process Rules	• *Management of micro-activities* • *Instructions (push)* • *Full information transparency*	• *Management of macro-entities (processes)* • *Incentives (pull)* • *Selective information visibility*
Business Process Renewal Approaches	• *Infrequent benchmarking* • *Infrequent reengineering (every 5-10 years)*	• *Continuous benchmarking* • *Dynamic reconfiguration*
Benefits	• *Experience effects* • *Diminishing returns*	• *Growing and continuous specialization* • *Increasing returns*

Source: John Hagel III and John Seely Brown, "Orchestrating Business Processes – Harnessing the Value of Web Services Technology," White Paper, 2002

Central to the open source solutions are shared standards, best practice functional requirements, and an unwavering commitment to state-of-the-art technology and systems development. The development of open source applications is a case study of VOI in action, reflecting the key attributes of communities of practice, collaborative development, leadership, and the intangible value of strategic innovation and collaborative leadership.

Business officers will do well to explore open source solutions as they come on the scene. In partnership with the technology leadership on campus, the business officer can help the institution evaluate the appropriate open source solutions to acquire.

One area of tremendous potential for open source applications is the domain of digital asset management. The Open Knowledge Initiative (OKI) and Open Courseware (OCW) program at MIT are pioneers in the sharing of knowledge objects and course materials. The development of institutional knowledge repositories such as those at OSU Knowledge Bank at Ohio State University and eScholarship at the University of California Digital Libraries are cases in point.

The pervasive deployment of loosely coupled applications will lead to the continuing deconstruction and reinvention of business processes.

Reinvention will operate in both directions: aggregation and disaggregation. Functional processes and services such as enrollment services will be aggregated at the same time that many supporting applications will be disaggregated and broken into loosely coupled, best-of-breed solutions. Both economies of scale and economies of skill will play a role. Many providers of best-of-breed applications will find new markets available to them. Resourceful colleges and universities or consortia that develop such applications may find customers at other institutions, corporations, governments, associations, and other nonprofits.

"As more and more of the routine operational activities of a company become automated, the task of turning them over to third-party providers becomes easier and more economical. Meanwhile, the reduction of business processes to digital form brings the company and its providers together, further reducing costs. Economies of skill will open up opportunities for incumbent companies to launch infraservice businesses that leverage the knowledge and information that have been acquired from one business to create value in a new and seemingly unrelated one."

Byron G. Auguste, Yvonne Hao, Marc Singer, and Michael Wiegand, "The Other Side of Outsourcing," The McKinsey Quarterly, 2002, Number 1, p.61-62.

"For the next-generation infrastructure to be viable, higher education institutions must hold themselves and vendors accountable for a new level of integration and cooperation."

Ed Lightfoot and Weldon Ihrig

Economies of Scale: Depend on cost saving delivered through scaling applications upward to ever-greater numbers of transactions.

Economies of Skill: Depend on skillful application and innovation to deliver value.

New Markets for Value: Web services will open up new markets for best-of-breed applications and knowledge.

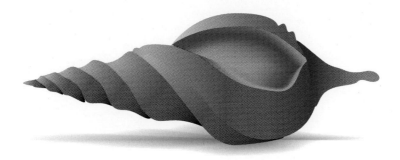

Applications from Value Chain to the Business Value Web

"To put it simply, the providers of infrastructures are successful when they manage to capture value that eludes their customer base."

Byron G. Auguste, Yvonne Hao, Marc Singer, and Michael Wiegand

When we combine Web services with loosely coupled organizations and business processes that expand beyond traditional enterprise boundaries, the potential exists for both ROI and VOI to increase dramatically. A new business model becomes possible, the business value web. In the business value web, value is released through the collaborative relationships. Traditional business processes are deconstructed. New business models are created that leverage integration and interoperable processes and systems.

The traditional value chain model needs to be supplemented and eventually replaced with a model that captures the richness and multi-dimensional characteristics we believe exist in the business value web framework. The traditional model represented in the figure below illustrates its linear, one-dimensional nature.

Value is represented as a series of relationships, transactions from "point a" to "point b." Components are serially and sequentially arrayed. The model clearly depicts many traditional business process relationships. It still has value to help represent elements of certain sales cycles, inventory management systems, manufacturing and supply chain systems, and the like.

Value Chain
Traditional, Tightly Coupled Organizations

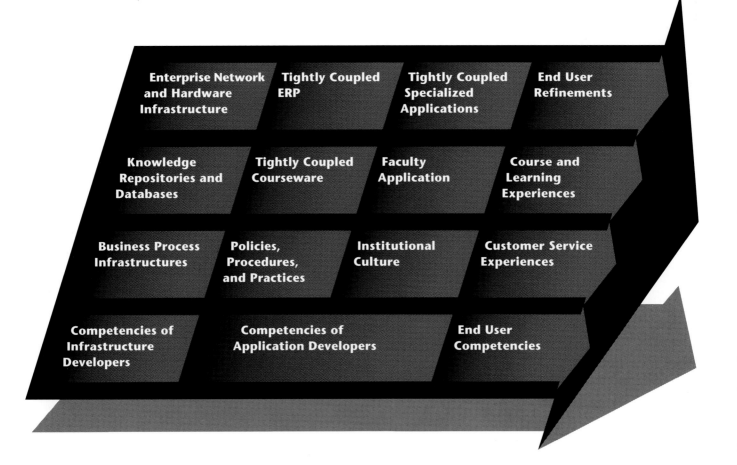

Business Value Web
Loosely Coupled Organizations

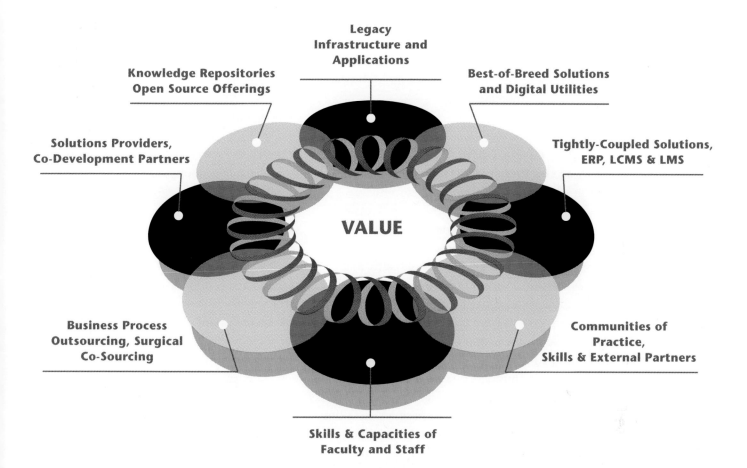

The traditional model is highly limited, however, in comparison with the potential of the business value web, which is based on a loosely coupled, multi-dimensional business process, with multiple partners, and new transitive trust relationships.

The framework of the business value web emphasizes the complex interplay between the business partners, the business process, the technology, and the transformation of fundamental business processes.

This robust model enables us to locate both ROI attributes and the strategic/intangible VOI aspects of business processes and practices. In such a framework, we can identify both the process issues that need to be considered and evaluated. We can also link the responsibility/"ownership" roles of the partners to the business relationship or transaction contemplated. Value now can be examined as it exists in the many dimensions of the model. New and innovative approaches to developing business solutions are encouraged by the business value web framework.

"As IT becomes an enabler of business agility and competitive advantage, we need to move the dialogue away from cost alone to the business value of IT."

Mohanbir Sawhney

The Business Officer's Emerging Responsibilities

The business officer is uniquely positioned to understand the entire institution's processes and how they fit together. In many ways, the business officer is like the conductor of an orchestra of business processes, shaping how they play together, their pace and loudness, and the framework through which they interoperate.

"The only way to predict the future is to have the power to shape the future."

Eric Hoffer

The Business Officer as Conductor of the Process Portfolio

Gradually, resourcing business processes and solutions is becoming a signature responsibility for campus business officers, working with multifunctional teams that combine a variety of academic and administrative perspectives. While business partnerships have always been a strategic issue for the institution, the range, variety and complexity of those relationships are growing. Business officers are becoming involved in the creation and management of a complex portfolio of business solutions that combine outsourced processes, sub-process "point" solutions, loosely coupled vendor products, and multi-faceted, co-created solutions. The portfolio is always "churning," with processes being combined, reinvented, deconstructed and disaggregated, and otherwise tweaked to optimize the value. The function of making strategic decisions on the portfolio of process solutions and on the supporting relationships will continue to move up the organizational hierarchy. At the same time, many particular process options will be analyzed and framed by teams drawn from front-line staff across the institution – or even multi-institutional teams such as those deployed by The Boston Consortium. These processes and analysis and selection will be transparent and open to comment.

The business process portfolio is always 'churning,' with processes being combined, reinvented, deconstructed, disaggregated, and otherwise changed to optimize value.

New Issues

The business officer is confronting a new series of key issues in dealing with the creation, management, and optimization of the portfolio of business processes and the elements of digital commerce:

- legal and contractual issues,
- digital signature,
- public key infrastructure (PKI) solutions,
- intellectual property rights,
- privacy,
- security,
- accountability and measurement, and
- affordability.

Accountability and measurement will figure prominently in these decisions. ROI and VOI will be important elements in deciding on technology investments. Both internal and external accountability will be important.

Linking Affordability and Accountability, ROI and VOI, Price and Cost

Consider for a moment the extraordinary pressures being placed on the campus in terms of the affordability crisis. Annual tuition increases regularly exceed standard inflation indices; the resulting public outcry is coupled with federal and state governments considering legislative solutions to the cost of college crisis. This creates a new order of challenges for business officers. Add to the mix the increased focus on issues of accountability, the governance implications of the Sarbanes-Oxley legislation, and the public focus on matters of trust, all creating complex considerations bedeviling all campus business officers. The business value web framework suggests approaches that can be used to grapple with these emerging challenges.

The figure below suggests the power of focusing on value, which encompasses cost, price, affordability, accountability, ROI, and VOI. Accountability and affordability are linked and understanding that relationship represents our increasing efforts at performance measurement. The "lens" through which we examine performance is "transparency," the watchword in corporate governance today. On one side, where accountability resides, we can place the ROI measures and characteristics of business valuation (tangible, measurable return). On the other end of the continuum, where affordability is located, VOI is central, and the focus is on intangibles and values of a strategic nature. The work of Kaplan and Norton on the "balanced scorecard" in fact is focused on just these measures of VOI attributes of a business model, while traditional financial accounting and reporting systems focus on very quantifiable, ROI kinds of measures. In 2001, NACUBO's national "Cost of College Study" examined and compared the differences between the *costs* of providing undergraduate education

and the *price* actually paid by the consumers. In all cases examined, the costs exceeded price, typically by more than 25 percent. "Cost" is quite measurable, accountable, and available to many ROI models and financial analytics. "Price" begins to get to issues of "affordability," which are inherently value-laden, subjective, and personal. As the figure illustrates, we move from the tactical aspects of business value to the strategic, and the model enables a rich and evocative analysis of complex systems and the inter-relationships of many dimensions.

The business value web framework provides the business officer with a valuable tool to array these several complex issues. In this way, one can begin to engage in a more informed dialogue and policy discussion with various stakeholders in the process: faculty, staff, students and their families, alumni, legislators, and other vested members of the higher education community.

> *"People-first organizations, not task-first ones, spawn hot groups that focus tirelessly on tasks."*
>
> *Harold J. Leavitt and Jean Lipman-Blumen*

Examining Affordability and Accountability

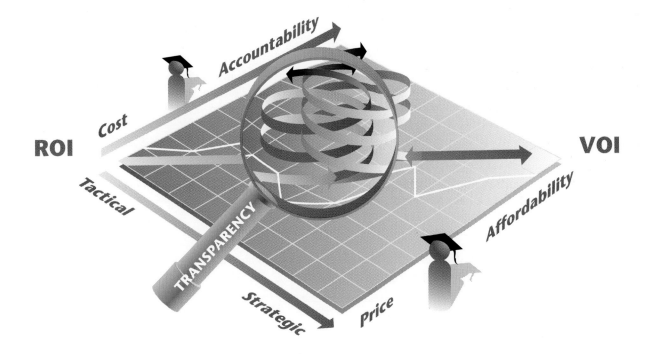

Using the Process Lens to Shape IT Decisions

In a recent article in the *Harvard Business Review*, Jeanne Ross and Peter Weill showcased "Six IT Decisions Your IT People Shouldn't Make." The point of the article was that strategic decisions about the allocation of IT resources to particular projects and accountability for results should not be made by IT decision-makers, operating in a vacuum.

Rather, these decisions should be driven by the enterprise's strategic objectives and held to strict standards of accountability. This ties in naturally with the notion of ROI and VOI. It is useful to focus on the contribution of IT investment to value and the resulting impact on competitive advantage. The business officer should help frame and focus such conversations, using the lens of the business process portfolio.

Six IT Decisions Your IT People Shouldn't Make

IT Decision	Senior Management's Role	Consequences of Abdicating the Decision
How much should we spend on IT?	Define the strategic role that IT will play and then determine the level of funding needed to achieve that objective.	The organization fails to develop an IT platform that furthers its strategy, despite high IT spending.
Which business processes should receive our IT dollars?	Make clear decisions about which IT initiatives will and will not be funded.	A lack of focus overwhelms the IT unit, which tries to deliver many projects that may have little organization-wide value or can't be implemented well simultaneously.
Which IT capabilities need to be organization-wide?	Decide which IT capabilities should be provided centrally and which should be developed by individual businesses.	Excessive technical and process standardization limits the flexibility of business units, or frequent exceptions to the standards increase costs and limit business synergies.
How good do our IT services really need to be?	Decide which features – for example, enhanced reliability or response time – are needed on the basis of their costs and benefits.	The organization may pay for service options that, given its priorities, aren't worth the costs.
What security and privacy risks will we accept?	Lead the decision making on the trade-offs between security and privacy on one hand and convenience on the other.	An overemphasis on security and privacy may inconvenience customers, employees, and suppliers; an underemphasis may make data vulnerable.
Whom do we blame if an IT initiative fails?	Assign a business executive to be accountable for every IT project; monitor business metrics.	The business value of systems is never realized.

Source: Jeanne W. Ross and Peter Weill, "Six IT Decisions Your IT People Shouldn't Make." Harvard Business Review, 2002, p. 7.

The Debate About Technology-Based Strategic Differentiation

In a controversial article in the May 2003 issue of the *Harvard Business Review*, Nicholas Carr argued that as information technology's power and ubiquity have grown, its strategic importance has diminished. He goes on to contend that IT is on its way to commoditization. Being highly replicable, IT is available to all and has lost its power as a strategic differentiator. Carr contends that enterprise leadership should work hard to control IT costs and reduce risks, rather than making significant investments in IT.

This article provoked a number of strong responses, including one from John Hagel III and John Seeley Brown, whose full letter appears in the July issue. Hagel and Brown observe that Carr's article captures the backlash sweeping through corporate officers against IT spending, prompted by disappointments with returns from IT investment. However, they believe that Carr misses the mark, because IT-based strategic differentiation is grounded on the following three principles:

- *Extracting business value from IT requires innovations in business practices.* IT alone provides no strategic advantage.

- *The economic impact from IT comes from incremental innovations, rather than big bang initiatives.* A process of rapid incrementalism enhances learning potential and creates opportunities for further innovations.

- *The strategic impact of IT investment comes from the cumulative effect of sustained initiatives to innovate business practices in the near term.* The strategic differentiation emerges over time, based less on any one specific innovation in business practice and much more on the capability to continuously innovate around the evolving capabilities of IT.

This debate further emphasizes the importance of focusing on business process reinvention and innovation in business practice. It affirms the necessity of asking tough questions about where value resides and how to enhance it. The business officer needs to figure prominently in this debate.

"We have yet to see a dominant architecture for IT emerge. We believe we are on the cusp of another major shift toward a truly distributed service architecture that will deliver a qualitative breakthrough in terms of delivering more flexibility and fluidity to businesses."

John Hagel III and John Seely Brown

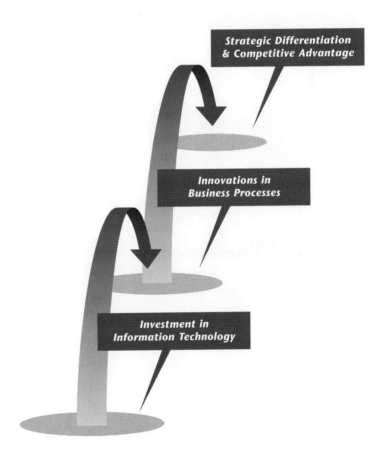

10 Initiatives to Improve Resourcing Decisions

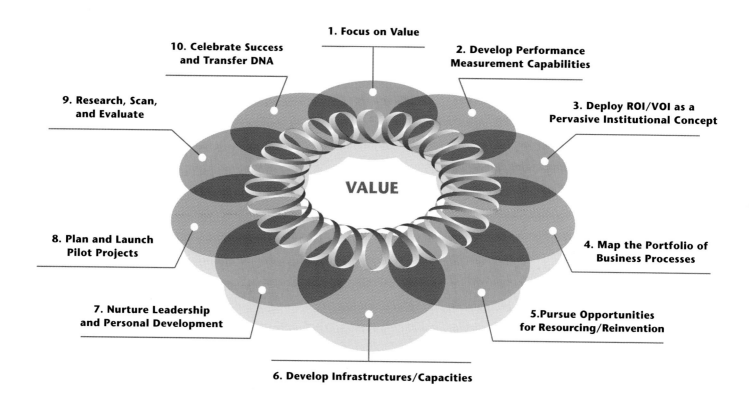

To thrive over the next decade, colleges and universities need to make a conscious commitment to enhancing the quality and managing the cost of higher education. Understanding and leveraging the business value web will be an important element of the business officer's tool kit. The building of a comprehensive resourcing perspective to business processes is a developmental process that requires the raising of perspectives and enhancement of competencies from the business officer down to the frontline customer service staff. These 10 initiatives are interconnected, parallel, and iterative, not sequential. This is not a 10-step process to self-improvement, but a enterprise-wide developmental effort involving individual, team, and organizational competencies.

To thrive over the next decade, colleges and universities need to make a conscious commitment to enhancing the quality of higher education and managing its cost. Understanding and leveraging the business value web is critical. This is a developmental process, not a 10-step process.

1. Focus on Value

The business officer should orchestrate the launching of a campus-wide dialogue on value – what it means, where it resides, and how to leverage it. The conversations about value should be in the context of real institutional processes and issues. It is effective to use storytelling to engage staff in how to enhance and optimize the value in their processes. Examples from leading-edge institutions are very helpful in establishing understanding. Explore how to leverage the business value web to establish competitive advantage, using cases to trigger conversations.

Understanding value and reflecting on how to enhance it should be everyone's job. The conversations should engage staff at all levels of the institution.

2. Develop Performance Measurement Capabilities

Develop the capacity of staff to use performance measurement to understand the cost and performance of campus processes – both academic and administrative. Discuss developing trends in transparency, accountability, and affordability. Engage the campus community in understanding these concepts and their implications for the institution's competitive position.

Most currently developed performance measures deal with ROI. Today, even leading innovators are at a stage where they can talk about VOI, but not really measure it. Understanding VOI and how to measure it must be developed over time. Attempting to use value measurement as a driver of decisions prematurely can thwart innovation. The Boston Consortium did not over-emphasize measurement of value in the early stages of development; instead it focused on ROI for derivative initiatives. VOI came later.

Whatever the progression, institutions will need to enhance their performance measurement capabilities dramatically. These will range from Institutional-level, macro-measurements to micro-measurement of the work flow and performance of individual processes or even parts of processes. Over time, activity-based costing will play a significant role.

3. Deploy ROI/VOI as a Pervasive Institutional Concept

As part of the ongoing conversation on value, discuss the relationship between ROI and VOI. Apply the metaphor of "two intersecting springs" to discuss how ROI and VOI are mutually reinforcing. Use real-life examples to illustrate ROI, VOI, and the impact of VOI on ROI over time. Use development of performance measurement capabilities to enhance understanding of ROI and VOI. Explore the roles of ROI and

VOI in linking tactics (ROI) and campus strategy (VOI). Understand how to use productivity enhancement, collaboration, and innovation to change the dynamics of processes and drive ever-greater VOI.

4. Map the Portfolio of Business Processes

The business officer should articulate the model of a portfolio of business processes as a means of focusing strategic decision-making at the cabinet level. This model should also encourage aggressive resourcing deliberations at the process level, using measures of mission criticality and performance to assess the campus portfolio of business processes on the evaluative matrix. The business officer should encourage and orchestrate lively discussion of opportunities to enhance performance of processes through combination, redesign, cost reduction, repricing, and/or elimination.

5. Pursue Opportunities for Resourcing/Reinvention

The metaphor of "perpetual churn" in the business process portfolio should also be encouraged. The business officers should orchestrate the identification and prioritization of a list of opportunities for new approaches to resourcing and process reinvention. She should deploy the whole range of process refinement options, select high priority candidates for resourcing initiatives, and proceed with them.

6. Develop Infrastructures/Capacities

Several kinds of infrastructures/capacities are essential: enterprise ICT infrastructure (network, enterprise applications, information management, communication), process applications, and the capacity of staff to utilize these infrastructures to support processes and measure performance. The business officer and staff need to be actively involved in strategic

"To paraphrase, the epicenter of knowledge may be with the individual, but the epicenter of leverage is with the organization."

Rudy Ruggles and Dan Holthouse

"In all affairs, love, religion, politics or business, it's a healthy idea, now and then to hang a question mark on things you have long taken for granted."

Bertrand Russell

"Storytelling, when linked directly to a company's strategic and cultural context, is a powerful means of simultaneously building strategic competence and strengthening organizational character."

Douglas Ready

"Envisioning the end is enough to put the means in motion."

Dorothea Brande

infrastructure development decisions and in decisions relating to individual process development. The business officer should consciously develop the infrastructures and capacities necessary to support process reinvention, resourcing, and innovation and encourage that these capacities be fully utilized.

A critical core competency is familiarity with the full range of resourcing options and relationships with a range of external solution providers. The business officer should work closely with the CIO to assure that these relationships are developed.

7. *Nurture Leadership and Personal Development*
Using his institution-wide perspective as a bully pulpit, the business officer should work with the campus executive team to place an institutional priority on the development of leadership and professional skills across the institution. He should consciously develop and hone the capacity of staff to engage in collaborative, innovative ventures. The best approach is to develop staff through participation in actual expeditionary ventures, continuously evaluating and sharing results.

Communities of practice are the best incubators of grassroots leadership. Turn existing teams and working groups into communities of reflective practice. Where possible, form communities of practice that extend beyond your institution. Let communities of practice develop from the bottom up. Give them plenty of rope, but engage them in conversations about what other communities have found. Let them determine the nature of the problems as well as the solutions.

8. *Plan and Launch Pilot Projects*
Pilot projects can emerge from communities of practice (preferred) or from the business officer. Use pilot projects to develop staff

capacities to problem solve, measure performance and results, and communicate learnings. Be certain to launch expeditionary projects that utilize combinations of Web services, shared services, BPO, reinvention, and other new techniques. Continuously monitor results, assess outcomes, provide feedback, and articulate how pilot projects are aligned with mission and vision.

9. *Research, Scan, and Evaluate*
Reflective practice is based on assessment of performance and comparison of performance with benchmarks, best practices, and other standards. The business officer should encourage environmental scanning, benchmarking, and research that reaches beyond the individual institution to include peer institutions, national standards, and other appropriate sources. Evaluation should be qualitative as well as quantitative.

10. *Celebrate Success and Transfer DNA*
Pilot projects, reinvention efforts, and resourcing initiatives should yield insights on what works. Such projects are expeditionary initiatives – probes into the future. The insights from successes and failures should be leveraged across the organization. Staff should engage in feedback and storytelling about what works and what doesn't, to increase the tradecraft of the communities of practice working on resourcing and reinvention initiatives.

The business officer should orchestrate a culture of reflective evaluation of the performance and effectiveness of campus business processes. The cultural DNA from successful projects should be assessed, understood, replicated, and injected into other processes and parts of the organization.

Vignette from the Future

What could a day in the life of a business officer be like in five years? Consider the following description of the roles, responsibilities, and perspectives in the not-so-distant future. The individual and the details of the institutional setting are hypothetical, but the conditions are based on today's realities, extrapolated several years into the future.

Carolyn Bodine
Chief Financial Officer
Bay State University

Carolyn Bodine assumed the CFO position at Bay State University three years ago, after joining the university in 2003 as associate CFO. She had been working at Boston Consortium institutions for 20 years, through which she had become acquainted with the leadership at Bay State and, in turn, they had observed her performance on several key initiatives.

President's Cabinet Reviews ICT Infrastructure Development and Process Enhancement.
Dr. Bodine just finished reviewing the minutes and action items from yesterday's president's cabinet meeting. She and the CIO had delivered a joint report on ICT infrastructure development and process enhancement plans. The report had been developed by a cross-functional working group that proposed institutional infrastructure investment based on VOI expectations. It also suggested specific process enhancements based on VOI and ROI expectations. The major strategic decision was not to replace the university's legacy student system with an ERP system. Rather, they would use the new portal developed using the uPortal product and Web services to create a loosely coupled architecture. Simultaneously, they have decided to resource a number of IT support services related to this project through a

solutions provider, in conjunction with three other institutions participating in The Boston Consortium.

Board of Trustees Reviews VOI and Affordability Indices.
The president's cabinet also approved the quarterly strategic VOI report, which would be shared with the board at its next meeting. Also on the board's agenda would be the annual benchmarking of Bay State against peer and national target institutions, based on affordability. Bodine maintains current and historical affordability benchmarks and checklists, which track tuition costs vs. the CPI, plus monitor and record reductions in cost. She also maps Bay State's progress against its stated, board-approved target of reducing tuition by 1 percent a year over the next 10 years, based on cost reduction, performance enhancement, and new sources of revenues. A special subcommittee of the board works with Dr. Bodine and her staff on this important issue.

Process Portfolio Working Group Refines Process Solutions.
This afternoon the CFO will meet with her Process Portfolio Working Group, which uses the four-quadrant model to map, measure, and monitor the resourcing status of Bay State's processes. New decisions are pending on three proposed process enhancements. First, the outsourced food services agreement is being revised, to include a number of additional food services-related auxiliary functions on which their solutions partner offered an attractive solution, in terms of both price and performance. Second, the mix of Enrollment Services functions has been consolidated into an integrated, cross-training staff unit at Bay State. Many of the processes have been deconstructed and are being provided by a combination of inhouse and surgically cosourced solutions.

Third, the e-learning Help Desk function is being outsourced to another institution in The Boston Consortium.

"As to the future, your task is not to foresee it, but to enable it."

Martin Gilbert

Digital Utilities and BPO Solutions Are a Valuable Alternative.

Bay State has been utilizing so-called digital utilities such at the National Student Clearinghouse for years. Recently, digital utility solutions to SEVIS have been offered, and the institution is evaluating several others. Tomorrow Dr. Bodine will be receiving BPO proposals from ACS, TMS, and several other firms regarding a variety of BPO opportunities in tuition management, financial aid services, human resources support, and telemarketing.

Activity-based Costing Working Group.

Two months ago, the CFOs at three Boston Consortium colleges and universities appointed a special working group to create a demonstration project on activity-based costing. This group is using workflow tools to model the productivity impacts of changes in processes, new personal productivity tools, and the training of front-line workers. This demonstration project will be used both to enhance productivity and as an instrument for developing staff. Activity-based costing tools are also being tested, so they can become a part of the affordability and productivity initiative. While Bay State is not participating, Carolyn Bodine is keen on tracking the results and considering Bay State's involvement in the future.

Three New Initiatives Recommended by Working Groups.

As she scans her virtual inbox, Dr. Bodine notes that three new initiatives have percolated upward from the The Boston Consortium working groups. The first concerns a new Pharmacy Carve Out opportunity; the private sector is finally making full-bodied pharmacy plans available. The second is a proposed initiative to consider expanding the Risk Management service to two additional Boston Consortium

institutions and two institutions that are considering joining the consortium and have asked to be able to sign up for risk management and pay an ASP fee. The third is adopting a BPO solution that will provide a full accounts payable service. Four additional initiatives are approaching the final review stage by The Boston Consortium's board and will be surfacing in her inbox over the next month.

Learning Histories Memorialize Insights, Lessons Learned, Mistakes Made.

Since becoming CFO, Dr. Bodine has created an online body of knowledge for the staff in her division. It draws from the Learning Histories developed by The Boston Consortium, reports and online logs from participants in working groups and initiative teams, and other sources. These materials are an important element in the ongoing development of staff. Contributions to the Learning Histories and capacity to participate effectively in the cross-institutional working groups are important elements in the evaluation of staff for promotional possibilities.

Stakeholder Service and Satisfaction Reports.

Bay State has been able to integrate new customer relationship management (CRM) capabilities into its portal. It has also used the portal to streamline and improve the experience stakeholders have in accessing the university's processes. Using these tools, Bay State is personalizing the online services to the needs of students, faculty and staff. It is also collecting a continuous stream of feedback on the satisfaction of students, faculty, and staff with its processes and suggestions for improvement. Bodine's Process Portfolio Working Group uses this stream of information as an integral element in monitoring the performance of BSU processes and identifying means of continuous improvement. Bodine has made continuous improvement an integral element of every Working Group's charge and an evaluative criteria for all staff in her division.

Knowledge Management and Learning Content Management Working Group. Dr. Bodine, the provost, and CIO, are scheduled to meet tomorrow to discuss the formation of a task force to assess the university's current state of development and future prospects in the use of learning management systems, learning content management systems, knowledge repositories, and open source initiatives such as the Open Knowledge Initiative and Open Courseware.

Preparation for CFO's Staff Retreat. Later this week, the CFO will meet with the director of human resources to plan for the upcoming CFO staff retreat   The retreat is organized as a developmental experience, but around a real-life task. The session will be led by a trained facilitator, using the The Boston Consortium approach, and focusing on one of three problem areas: 1) using a fully integrated risk management function (risk management, internal audit, and legal affairs) to systematically reduce the university's risk exposure and generate real cost savings and performance enhancement; 2) investigating shared athletic and recreational facilities with two institutions located within two miles of Bay State University, plus the local township; and 3) reviewing the implications of changes in FASB/GASB standards, state reporting requirements, and other regulations on institutional reporting and accountability.

Five phone calls, three Web conferences, and an hour of answering e-mail later, it was nearly the end of the day. In 10 minutes, the CFO will caucus with her staff assistant to review plans for the rest of the week.

"It may now make more sense to talk about a company's distributed capabilities instead of core capabilities."

Mohanbir Sawnhey and Deval Parikh

"The future is like heaven. Everybody exalts it, but nobody wants to go there now."

James Baldwin

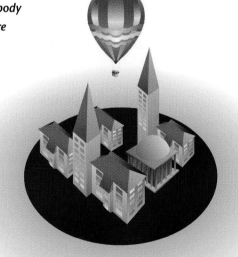

Leadership, Innovation, and Reinvention

Higher education has confronted some dramatic challenges over the past 60 years. Each has required concerted leadership and marshalling of energies and resources. Most dealt with growth, but some wrestled with retrenchment. Many have required the development of new models and practices. However, none of these challenges occurred in a context of declining public support for education funding and the changing dynamics of globalization and the Knowledge Economy. Moreover, none required the combination of leadership, creativity, innovation, reinvention, and rapid response that will be expected of institutional leadership over the next five years.

A Call for Leadership

The next few years will not be about the management of decline, unless we experience a failure in leadership. Our future should be about reinventing higher education, institution by institution, and in collaboration with others. Succeeding in tough times will require big choices and strong leadership. It will also require a keener interest in innovation than has been rewarded in our past. And it will require a more sophisticated, pervasive development of the competencies of staff, faculty, suppliers, and other stakeholders.

New Tools and Perspectives

The business value web could serve as an essential instrument for institutions that successfully confront these challenges. Resourcing business processes and solutions in new and creative ways will be a central challenge and opportunity for many chief financial officers (CFOs) and chief business officers (CBOs). They will be called upon to play a critical leadership role in orchestrating new approaches to resourcing and process reinvention, in partnership with other senior campus executives.

Collaboration and Innovation As Distributed Competencies

The most important lesson to be drawn from the case studies is that successful resourcing requires collaboration on campus within and among staffs and working groups, external solution partners, professionals at other institutions, and other sources of expertise. Colleges and universities need to develop their competencies in collaboration and innovation not as "core" competencies, but as "distributed" competencies. These competencies must be distributed across the institution, from executive leadership to grassroots. And the sources of expertise must be distributed through formal and informal communities of reflective practice that span organizational and institutional borders.

Reconciling Collaboration and Sharing with Building Competitive Advantage

We began with the proposition that enhancing value for an institution's stakeholders translates into competitive advantage. Does competition contradict the power of collaboration? Sharing of insight with other institutions would diminish an institution's competitive standing if innovation were a "zero sum game." However, innovation in higher education feeds upon collaboration and exchange of insight. Moreover, one of our great challenges is to restore public trust in higher education, which has been eroded over the past decade. This will require enhancing the value dimension for a broad cross section of American higher education, not just a cadre of leading innovators.

Put simply, *The Business Value Web* offers the necessary support for enhancing the distributed capacity of American higher education to collaborate, innovate, and create a more attractive value proposition for its stakeholders.

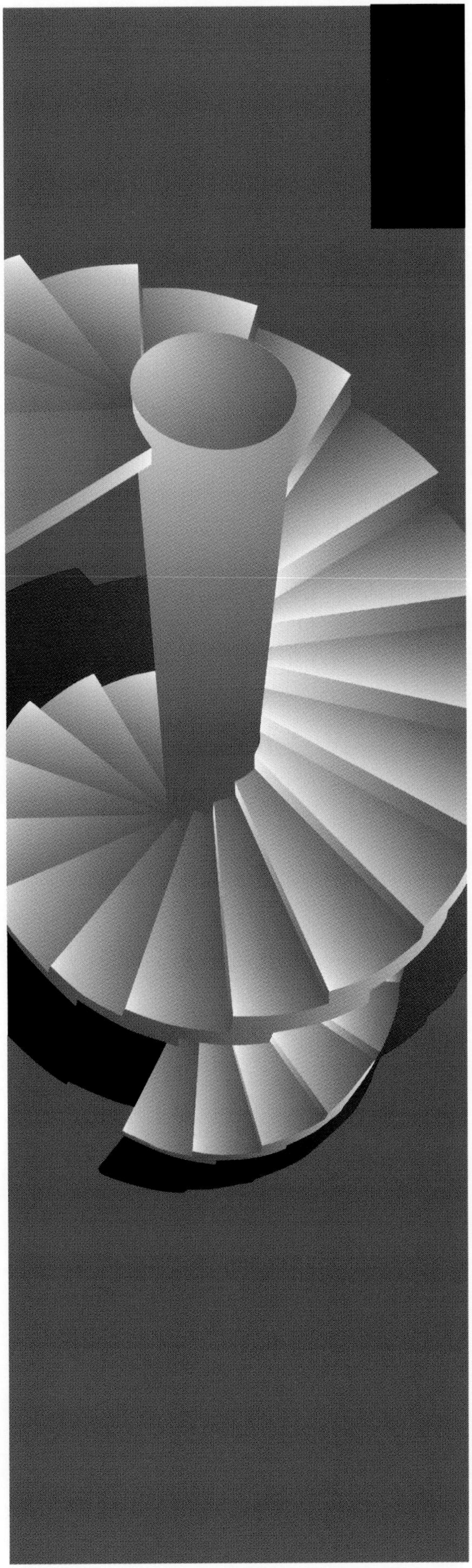

Bibliography

A set of bibliographic materials is provided to guide further research on this subject.

Bibliography

Auguste, Byron G., Yvonne Hao, Marc Singer, and Michael Wiegand. "The Other Side of Outsourcing," *McKinsey Quarterly*, Number 1, 2002.

Baker, Hugh and Tim Laseter. "The Four Phases of Continuous Sourcing," *Strategy+Business*, Issue 27, pp. 32-37.

Barone, Carole A. "WINWINI and the Next Killer App – an Interview with Carl F. Berger," *EDUCAUSE Review*, March/April 2002, pp. 21-26.

Beach, Gary J. "ROI Is DOA," *CIO*, April 1, 2002, p. 98.

Bender, Walter. "Twenty Years of Personalization: All About the 'Daily Me,'" *EDUCAUSE Review*, September/October 2002, pp. 20-29.

Berkman, Eric. "How to Use the Balanced Scorecard," *CIO*, May 15, 2002, pp. 93-100.

Blumenstyk, Goldie. "Technology 'Outsourcing': The Results Are Mixed," *Chronicle of Higher Education*, October 29, 1999.

Boettcher, Judith V., Robert Brentrup, and John Douglass. "Digital Certificates: Coming of Age," *EDUCAUSE Review*, January/February 2003.

Brown, John Seely, Scott Durschlag, and John Hagel III. "Loosening Up: How Process Networks Unlock the Power of Specialization," *McKinsey Quarterly*, Number 2, 2002.

Carr, Nicholas. "IT Doesn't Matter," *Harvard Business Review*, May 2003.

Christensen, Clayton M., Sally Aaron, and William Clark. "Disruption in Education," *EDUCAUSE Review*, January/February 2003, pp. 44-54.

Chronicle of Higher Education. "10 Ways Colleges Can Cut IT Costs," *Chronicle of Higher Education*, September 30, 2002.

Chung, Anne, Tim Jackson and Tim Laseter. "Why Outsourcing Is In," *Strategy + Business*, Issue 28, pp. 22-27.

Clinton, Patrick. "Technology Purchasing," *University Business*, July 28, 2002.

Collins, Jim. "*Good to Great: Why Some Companies Make the Leap... and Others Don't,*" New York: HarperBusiness, 2001.

Cramm, Susan H. "The Dark Side of Outsourcing," *CIO*, November 15, 2001.

Datz, Todd. "Big (And Not So Big) Ideas for 2003," *CIO*, January 1, 2003.

Engardio, Pete, Aaron Bernstein, and Manjeet Kripalani. "Is Your Job Next?" *BusinessWeek*, February 3, 2003, pp. 50-60.

Frantz, Pollyanne S., Arthur R. Southerland, and James T. Johnson. "ERP Software Implementation Best Practices," *EDUCAUSE Quarterly*, Number 4, 2002, pp. 38-45.

Gartner. "What Web Services Won't Do," *Gartner Research Note,* February 19, 2002.

Gartner. *Strategic Sourcing: The Book.* 2002.

Gartner. "Changing the View of ROI to VOI – Value on Investment," *Gartner Research Note,* 14 November 2001.

Barone's and Bender's articles on portalization and personalization are important to understanding the portal as a gateway to experiences, resources, programs, and services.

Christensen, Aaron, and Clark's article on disruption in education suggests how truly disruptive offerings may challenge traditional education offerings in distance learning and professional education.

Gartner. "ROI and the E-Business Portfolio," *Research Note, Strategic Planning Assumption,* December 3, 1999.

Gleason, Bernard W. "Integrating to the Max," *NACUBO Business Officer,* September 2002, pp. 28-36.

Gleason, Bernard W. "Web Services in Higher Education – Hype, Reality, Opportunities," *EDUCAUSE Quarterly,* Number 3, 2002, pp. 11-13.

Glick, Milton and Jane Kupiec. "The Answer Is Still Technology: Strategic Technology," *EDUCAUSE Review,* November/December 2001, pp.32-3.

Goral, Tom. "50 Smart Business Improvements for 2003," *University Business,* December 17, 2002.

Graves, William H. "New Educational Wealth as a Return on Investment in Technology," *EDUCAUSE Review,* July/August 2002, pp.38-47.

Grayson, Katherine. "Meeting the Competition: Inside Brown University's Future's Project," *University Business,* December 4, 2002.

Guskin, Alan E. and Mary B. Marcy. "Dealing with the Future Now: Principles for Creating a Vital Campus in a Climate of Restricted Resources," *Change,* July/August 2003, pp. 10-21.

Hagel, John III and John Seeley Brown. *"Control vs. Trust – Mastering a Different Management Approach,"* White Paper, 2002.

Hagel, John III and John Seeley Brown. *"Orchestrating Business Processes – Harnessing the Value of Web Services Technology,"* White Paper, 2002.

Hagel, John III and John Seely Brown. Letter to the editor, *Harvard Business Review,* July 2003. A condensed version of this response to Carr is contained on Hagel's Weblog at (http://www.johnhagel.com/blog20030515.html)

Hagel, John III and John Seeley Brown. "Your Next IT Strategy," *Harvard Business Review,* October 2001, pp. 105 – 113.

Hagel, John III and John Seeley Brown. *"Service Grids: The Missing Link in Web Services,"* White Paper, 2002.

Hagel, John III, Scott Durschlag, and John Seely Brown. *"Orchestrating Loosely Coupled Business Processes: The Secret to Successful Collaboration,"* White Paper, 2002.

Hagel, John, III. *"Out of the Box: Strategies for Achieving Profits Today and Growth Tomorrow Through Web Services,"* Boston: Harvard Business School Press, Forthcoming.

Hagel, John III. "Leveraged Growth: Expanding Sales without Sacrificing Profits," *Harvard Business Review,* October 2002, pp. 69-77.

Hammonds, Keith H. "Smart, Ambitious, Cheap: The New Face of Global Competition," *Fast Company,* February 2003, pp. 91-97.

Harris, K., M. Gray and C. Rozwell. "Changing the View of ROI to VOI – Value on Investment," *Gartner Research Note, Strategic Planning,* SPA-14-7250, November 14, 2001.

Hoffman, Thomas. "Big Shift in IT Jobs to Outsourcing Predicted," *Computerworld,* January 24, 2003.

Gleason's articles are important for their focus on transitive trust and Web services developments.

John Hagel III and John Seeley Brown's work on loosely coupled applications and services are must read in understanding the emerging application, process, and solution environment.

ECAR's research studies on outsourcing and ERP are critical to understanding current and future states of development in these important areas.

Hoffman, Thomas. "Q&A: John Hagel on the Business Impact of Web Services," *Computerworld,* November 14, 2002.

Hyder, Elaine et al. "The Capability Model for IT-enabled Outsourcing Service Providers," *White Paper: School of Computer Science, Carnegie Mellon University,* 2002.

Jacobson, Carl. "Web Services: Stitching Together the Institutional Fabric," *EDUCAUSE Review,* March/April 2002, pp. 50-51.

Kaganoff, Tessa. "Collaboration, Technology, and Outsourcing: Initiatives in Higher Education: A Literature Review," *RAND,* 1998.

Kalin, Sari. "Return on Investment," *CIO,* August 15, 2002, pp. 75-80.

Katz, Richard. "The ICT Infrastructure: Driver of Change," *EDUCAUSE Review,* July/August 2002, pp. 50-61.

Lightfoot and Ihrig's article illuminates the nature of next generation technology infrastructures.

Keen, Jack M. and Bonnie Digrius. "The Emotional Enigma of Intangibles," *CIO,* February 15, 2003.

Koch, Christopher. "Why Your Integration Efforts End Up Looking Like This," *CIO,* November 15, 2002, pp. 98-108.

Koch, Christopher. "Enterprise Software Upgrades: Less Pain, More Gain," *CIO,* November 15, 2002, pp. 46-56.

Koch, Christopher. "It's Time to Take Control," *CIO,* July 15, 2002, pp. 46-52.

Kvavik, Robert B. and Richard N. Katz. "The Promise and Performance of Enterprise Systems for Higher Education," *Boulder: ECAR,* Volume 4, 2002.

Kvavik, Robert B. and Michael N. Handberg. "Transforming Student Services: The University of Minnesota Takes a Fresh Look at Client/Institution Interaction," *Educause Quarterly,* Volume 23, Number 2, 2000, pp. 30 – 37.

Lightfoot, Ed and Weldon Ihrig. "The Next-Generation Infrastructure," *EDUCAUSE Review,* November/December 2002, pp. 52-61.

Lohmeyer, Dan, Sofya Pogreb, and Scott Robinson. "Who's Accountable for IT?" *McKinsey Quarterly,* December 19, 2002.

Lohr, Steve. "Competitors Shape Strategy to Gain Edge in Web Services," *The New York Times,* February 3, 2003.

Lorenzo, George. *"Web Services Enabling Technology for Application Integration and Assembly,"* Commissioned White Paper: Hekate and SCT, July 2002.

Manasian, David. "Digital Dilemmas: A Survey of the Internet Society," *The Economist,* January 25, 2003, pp. 1-26.

Mayor, Tracy. "A Buyer's Guide to I.T. Value Methodologies," *CIO,* July 15, 2002, pp. 60-68.

McCollum, Kelly. "Colleges Struggle to Manage Technology's Rising Costs," *Chronicle of Higher Education,* February 19, 1999.

Mercer, Joyce. "Contracting Out: Colleges Are Turning to Private Vendors for More and More Campus Services," *Chronicle of Higher Education,* July 7, 1995, pp. 37-38.

McCord, Alan. "Are You Ready to Discuss IT Outsourcing on Your Campus?" *EDUCAUSE Quarterly,* Number 1, 2002, pp. 12-19.

Murray, Kevin. "Now Is the Time to Pull the Plug on Your Legacy Apps," *CIO*, March 15, 2002, pp.56-64.

McKenzie, Ross. "Strategic Partnering and New Technology," *EDUCAUSE Quarterly*, November 4, 2002.

National Association of College Auxiliary Services. *"Privatization of Campus Housing in Higher Education: Papers and Presentations,"* Charlottesville, VA: NACAS, 1997.

Nee, Eric. "Webware for Rent," *Fortune*, September 6, 1999, pp. 215-224.

Norris, Donald M. "Expanding ROI to VOI for E-Procurement," *Purchasing Pulse*, December 2001.

Norris, Donald M. *"Assuring Value from Your Technology Investment,"* Forthcoming.

Norris, Donald, Jon Mason and Paul Lefere. *"Transforming e-Knowledge: A Revolution in the Sharing of Knowledge,"* Ann Arbor: Society for College and University Planning, 2003.

Olsen, Florence. "As Ever, Computing Officials Ask: Build or Buy?" *Chronicle of Higher Education*, June 2, 2000.

Olsen, Florence. "Service from Sallie Mae's New Division Lets Students Pay Their Tuition Bills Online," *Chronicle of Higher Education*, June 9, 2000.

Olson, Mark A. *"Strategic Imperatives: The Business of Information Technology,"* March 26, 2002.

Overby, Susan. "This Could Be the Start of Something Small," *CIO*, February 15, 2003, pp. 55-62.

Patton, Susan. "Web Metrics That Matter," *CIO*, November 15, 2002, pp. 84-88.

Quinn, James Brian. "Services and Technology: Revolutionizing Higher Education," *EDUCAUSE Review.*

Rivard, Nicole. "Selling for Fun and Profit," *University Business*, May 2, 2003.

Ross, Jeanne W. and Peter Weill. "Six Decisions Your IT People Shouldn't Make," *Harvard Business Review*, November 2002, pp. 85-91.

Savarese, John. "To Outsource, or Not to Outsource... This is the IT question so many schools are asking right now," *University Business*, January 30, 2003.

Sawhney, Mohanbir. "Dam the ROI, Full Speed Ahead," *CIO*, July 15, 2002, pp. 36-38.

Sawhney, Mohanbir. "Fundamentals of Value," *CIO*, July 1, 2003, pp. 34-36.

Sederburg, William A. "The Net-Enhanced University," *EDUCAUSE Review*, September/October 2002, pp.64-72.

Seikman, Philip. "Outsourcing Is More Than Cost Cutting," *Fortune*, October 26, 1998, pp. 238C-V.

Sim, Stephanie. "Gartner: IT services market to be worth $865B by 2005," *Computerworld*, December 27, 2001.

Smallen, David and Karen Leach. "7 Benchmarks for Information Technology Investment," *EDUCAUSE Quarterly*, Number 3, 2002, pp. 22-27.

Strauss, Howard. "The Right Train at the Right Station," *EDUCAUSE Review*, May/June 2002, pp.30-36.

Sunstein, Cass R. "MyUniversity.com," *EDUCAUSE Review*, September/October 2002.

Ross and Weill's article focuses on the importance of linking ICT decisions to process enhancement and business process goals.

Turk's article on resourcing is a classic that should be revisited.

Thornton, Tom. "Think Carefully When Looking at Outsourcing," *INFOTECH Executive,* May 23, 2002.

Turk, Frederick J. "After Re-engineering Comes Resourcing," *NACUBO Business Officer,* August 1998.

Twigg, Carol A. "Getting Results from Investments in Technology," *AGB Priorities,* Spring 1999.

Varon, Elana. "Strategic Portals Gets Down to Business," *CIO,* December 1, 2002, pp. 70-76.

Weir, Bob and Rick Mickool. "For Enterprise Applications and Data, the Question Is Not Make Versus Buy..." *EDUCAUSE Quarterly,* Number 1, 2003, pp. 5-15.

Wenger, Etienne, Richard McDermott, and William M. Snyder. *"Cultivating Communities of Practice,"* Cambridge: Harvard Business School Press, 2002.

Wertz's work on privatization and outsourcing of campus services captures the current state of practice.

Wertz, Richard. *"Privatization Survey Summary,"* Charlottesville, VA: NACAS, 1997.

Wertz, Richard. *"Outsourcing and Privatization of Campus Services: An Overview and Guide for College and University Administrators,"* Charlottesville, VA: NACAS, 1997.

Wertz, Richard and Sennis Gribinas. *"Privatization of Campus Services at Community Colleges in the United States,"* Charlottesville, VA: NACAS, 1998.

Wood, Patricia A. "Outsourcing in Higher Education," *ERIC Higher Education Digest Series,* 2000.

Worthen, Ben. "Web Services: Still Not Ready for Prime Time," *CIO,* September 1, 2002, pp. 72-76.

Wulf, William A. "Higher Education Alert: The Information Railroad Is Coming," *EDUCAUSE Review,* January/February 2003, pp. 12-21.

Yanosky, R. "Higher-Education Enterprise Portals: Vertical to Verticalized," *Research Note, Markets,* M-15-0778, 14 January 2002.

Zastrocky, Michael. "Best Practices in Selecting and Implementing a Student Information System," *Gartner Group Presentation.*

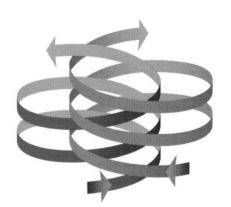